# PRAISE FOR
## . . . THE CAR BUYER'S ART . . .

. . . Will teach you the rules of bare knuckle bargaining"

**U.S. NEWS & WORLD REPORT**

Your interview about buying a car was most informative—YOU WERE GREAT!

**THE CNN TELEVISION NETWORK**

You have a good product, and a timely one.

**CONSUMER REPORTS**

This is definitely not just another boring How-to-Buy-A-Car effort

**Editor of THE CO-EVOLUTION QUARTERLY**

An extremely practical study of the bargaining techniques and psychological leverages employed in coping with a used-car dealer

**LOS ANGELES TIMES**

Promotes strategies that car buyers can use to counter most of the really devious sales schemes.

**UNITED PRESS INTERNATIONAL**

Special Report: How To Buy A Car . . . Ex-salesman warns buyers of pitfalls . . .

**USA TODAY**

ADVISES PROSPECTS HOW TO PAY A "fair" price for a new car by giving them an insider's LOOK AT THE SELLING PROCESS . . .

**WARD'S AUTO WORLD**

You can play the car wars game and keep your shirt, but first, you must know the rules.

**THE DAILY NEWS**

I know it's a typical sticker-shock reaction, Parrish, but, my gosh, he works here!

**Cartoonist, THE CHICAGO TRIBUNE**

This book is written in a breezy, entertaining style, but for those who care to take the time to digest it carefully, there are valuable lessons to be learned which can save the reader a great deal of money.

**RETIREMENT LIFE**

That apotheosis of the hard sell, the car salesman, finally may have met his match.

**THE ARIZONA REPUBLIC**

Inside information, strategies and psychology help you thwart the sales tricks. . .

**Washington, D.C., CHANGING TIMES**

. . . THE CAR BUYER'S ART . . . can be as valuable to a car buyer as having a relative in the auto biz.

**TUCSON CITIZEN**

It's a book filled with extremely helpful consumer advice with very little superfluous self-congratulatory tales that often mark this type of book.

**Long Beach PRESS-TELEGRAM**

Darrell Parrish is a traitor to his former profession: selling cars. He has turned on his old colleagues and revealed the secrets ad psychological games as they transpire during the selling of a car.

**Torrance, California DAILY BREEZE**

Parrish is to car dealers now what Serpico was to the New York Police Department . . .

**DAILY FORTY-NINER**

'That's it! You've ruined the market!

**A car dealer's son, after attending a
Parrish Seminar on car buying.**

# THE CAR BUYER'S ART

### . . . How to Beat the Salesman at His Own Game

Darrell Parrish

*Illustrations by Don Hillman*

**BOOK EXPRESS**
Publisher

P.O. Box 1249
Bellflower, California 90706
(213) 867-3723

Copyright © 1989
by
DARRELL BRUCE PARRISH

PREVIOUS EDITIONS
1985 by D.B. Parrish
1981 by D. Parrish & R. DiZazzo

ISBN 0-9612322-1-8
Library of Congress Cataloguing in Publication Data

Parrish, Darrell Bruce, 1946
The Car Buyer's Art—*How to Beat the Salesman at His Own Game.*
1. Title          I. Consumer Research

| | |
|---|---|
| 2nd Printing | 4th Printing |
| 3rd Printing | 5th Printing |
| 4th Printing | REVISED EDITION  1989 |
| REVISED EDITION 1985 | |
| 2nd Printing | |
| 3rd Printing | |

BOOK EXPRESS
P.O. BOX 1249
BELLFLOWER, CALIFORNIA 90706
(213) 867-3723

# CONTENTS

## CAR BUYER'S BASIC TRAINING SECTION

**ADVANCED CAR BUYER'S INDIVIDUAL TRAINING SECTION**

# ACKNOWLEDGMENTS

I wish to thank the following people who helped make this book possible, some inspirational, some who provided valuable information and guidance, and some technical expertise. I am greatly indebted to my wife Barbara, for her encouragement and support, to Dr. Robert Rheinish and Dr. William Buckner of California State University of Long Beach, and especially to the Home Economics Department of that institution for sponsoring my lectures and seminars. To early students who applied *The Car Buyer's Art* principles to their existing buying methods and illustrated to me that big savings can be pocketed easily, in cash, if only we dare to ask! To Mr. Richard L. Chan for his counsel. And to America's radio/television producers & hosts concerned with their audience's interest and freedom to allow expression of one's beliefs and ideas, a special salute!

Darrell Parrish
1985

# PUBLISHER'S NOTE

This book is sold with the understanding that neither the author nor the publisher is engaged in rendering legal or accounting advice or services. Questions relevant to the practice of law or accounting should be addressed to a member of those professions.

The author and the publisher specifically disclaim any liability, loss, or risk, personal or otherwise, incurred as a consequence, directly or indirectly, of the use and application of any of the contents of this work. The author stresses the reader should not take this material lightly and that only the *diligent reader safeguards maximum savings.* After several uses of **THE CAR BUYER'S ART**, this book will become common knowledge to its user. It's an honor to make this book available to the public and in the hope that it will generate more "artistic" car buyers in **America**.

I would like to dedicate the book you are about to read to two groups of people: consumers and car salesmen.

If you are one of the vast majority of consumers who needlessly hand millions of dollars in excess profit to new car dealerships and lots yearly, I offer the book to you as a tool. With its diligent use by you and large numbers of other car buyers, you can be assured that excess million dollars figure will suddenly take an enormous drop. What's more, hundreds, and in some cases *thousands*, of those dollars will drop into *your* bank account! In addition, you will find that for the first time in your life the act of buying a car will become, not the dreaded chore you may once have considered it, but rather an exciting and challenging accomplishment—one of which you can be proud. I know. I have seen and done it myself!

And that brings us to our next group—the car salesmen of America—perhaps the world's most infamous group of fast-talking, patent leather foxes. You, I must address in two categories: the honest and the dishonest.

For those who fall into the former category, your job will now become much more challenging and, in turn, rewarding. For the artistic buyer will never be easy. During a bargaining session he will stay with you, tooth and nail, to the end. In a word, he will know a fair deal when he sees one and know how to get it. And it is only from this kind of an encounter that you will both come away with a sense of satisfaction and mutual respect for each other.

As for those salesmen who fall into the latter category, I can only say this: if up to now you have made a living taking car buyers "for a ride," today just might be the day to start considering a new profession . . .

DARRELL PARRISH

*I dedicate this work to my grandson DANIEL. A living treasure to my heart.*

D.P.

# CHAPTER ONE

# 1
# LEGEND OF THE LOTS

Selling cars may not be the noblest art in the world, but an art it truly is—complete with an intricate and extremely effective set of working disciplines.

The man who sells cars, if he is to be successful, must logically, then, become an artist. His talents must be both numerous and diverse. He must be a quick-thinking mathematician and an amateur psychologist, a shrewd businessman and an accomplished actor. Needless to say, he must also be a persuasive talker—a man who can cajole, humor or if necessary for the "good" of his deal, become belligerent and insulting. The car salesman's foremost talent, though, is that one commanding trait which encompasses nearly all other criteria—his ability to know people. When involved in a bargaining session, he must not only be able to spot the most insignificant signs of fear and in decision in the buyer, but he must be able to capitalize on them at once—taking control, leading his unsuspecting consumer through a planned sequence of events which in the end will relieve the buyer of the maximum amount of dollars in exchange for an automobile.

So accomplished has the typical car salesman become at this, that he has become a legend in his own time. We envision him on the sprawling lot, waiting with greedy impatience among the rows of immaculately polished cars. We tell ourselves before stepping onto the lot that he is ruthless, heartless, a fast-talking flashy dresser with dollar signs in his eyes and a diamond ring on every finger.

Some time ago, shortly after becoming a car salesman, a question occurred to me. *Why, if the average man or woman on the street sees the typical car salesman as a portrait of dishonesty, is the salesman nonetheless able to extract the buyer's money with such seeming ease?* It didn't take long in the business to realize that the answer was simple. The typical buyer steps onto the car salesman's turf—the emotionally charged, dog-eat-dog world of retail car selling—without ever realizing there is also an art to *buying* a car! It is an art which requires an equally intricate set of working disciplines and, as I have personally found out (from the seller's end of the deal), one which is equally effective.

Let me now relate a story in a nutshell:

Several years ago, while selling cars for a large dealership in Southern California, I had the misfortune of entering into a bargaining session with a shrewd woman whom I'll call Ms. Stone. Soon after our conversation began, it became evident Ms. Stone was going to be a tough customer. It wasn't until we had completed all the preliminary steps and entered my office to begin the *real bargaining* that I found out how tough. My normal commission on the deal we were talking about should have been upwards of $ 180.00 (20% of total profit). Three gruelling hours later, when Ms. Stone had finished with me (and I mean that literally), I had settled for a hard fought $21.50 (The dealership got $103.00)! And I felt fortunate to have squeezed that out of the deal!

Why was Ms. Stone able to "head me off" at every turn and eventually corner me into a position where the dealer and I had no choice but to "give the car away" at "pennies" over our cost? Again, the answer is simple. She knew the buyer's art. She said and did exactly the *right* things at exactly the right times. She knew car prices, trade-in values and terms. She had also planned the deal she wanted in advance and was confident if she played her cards *right* she would get it!

But even aside from all of Ms. Stone's apparent car buyer's knowledge, there was another factor not apparent to me at the time, that played an important part in her effectiveness at bargaining for automobiles—simply the fact she was a woman!

To clarify this, let me return for a moment to the subject of "legendary" images. Just as most buyers envision car salesmen as notorious con-men, salesmen in turn categorize people into "typical" buyer categories. During my time as a salesman I termed the most common of these the "typically uninformed buyer," that vast majority of people who every day get taken for a ride, so to speak, simply because they don't know the "mechanics" of such things as wholesale and retail prices, terms, my goals as a salesman and the techniques I used time and again for achieving those goals. And as if this lack of information weren't enough, "typically uninformed buyers" tended to display other common weaknesses. As a rule they were indecisive, wary, impulsive and, as a result, easily mislead.

Now take a guess as to which gender of the species (placed at the top of this "typically easy to mislead" category? You guessed it—women. For who should know less about buying cars than the average woman, right? It was *exactly* this type of "typical" thinking on my part that, unknown to me at the time, gave Ms. Stone an additional powerful "hidden" advantage. She knew perfectly well that as a "typical" car salesman, I would have a difficult time dealing with a woman who didn't fit into the category she was supposed to. And how right she was!

It is with the spirit of this wonderfully *crafty* woman and those few other "artistic buyers" I've had the pleasure of dealing with during my time as a car salesman, that I have written THE CAR BUYER'S ART—HOW TO BEAT THE SALES-MAN AT HIS OWN GAME! In doing so, I have attempted to make available to you all the information needed to become a Mr. or Ms. Stone yourself.

Topics range from the basic workings of car dealerships to specific firing line techniques designed to use against that most formidable of adversaries—**the salesman himself.**

And exactly how can learning the car buyer's art benefit you? Let's look at a brief example. The average buyer, when purchasing a $10,000 car will normally leave the dealership with at least 20% ($2,000) profit when considering the *entire* deal. If he or she trades in a late model automobile with a wholesale value of $5,000, the dealership will, in almost every case, literally "steal" it for a much lower figure of around $3,000. They (dealership) will then do minor service work on it, turn around and attempt to sell it, (possibly as is) not for the $5,000 wholesale value, but for an inflated retail value of $6,500! The result? A $2,000 loss in trade-in equity for the buyer and a whopping $3,500 profit (ideal situation) for the dealership! If this same buyer finances through the dealership and is "typically" unaware of loan terms and options available, the dealer can easily capture another 3-5% profit on the amount financed. If that amount is $8,000 that's another $400. Now, let's do a little simple math:

| | |
|---:|---|
| $2,000 | Profit on new car sale |
| 2,000 | Profit on trade-in equity |
| 400 | Profit on amount financed |
| $4,400 | Total profit from "typical" sale |

Not a drop in the bucket by any means. With an artistic buyer, however, it's a different story. The profit margin on the new car sale, for instance, will be preplanned by the artistic buyer at somewhere between 5 and 10%. If, continuing with our previous example, we split the difference and make it 7% on that same $10,000 car, the $2,000 profit figure suddenly drops to $700. As for the trade-in, the artistic buyer will plan, demand and get top dollar for his trade-in (wholesale), thereby reducing this profit figure (equity loss) to a much more reasonable figure of around $250. And as for financing, you can't borrow money without paying interest (profit) to someone, but the artistic buyer will work it out so the dealership will get (if anything at all) a minimum of 1 or 2%,—or about $200 of that potential profit. Now let's see how both sets of figures compare:

| Typical car buy | | Artistic car buy |
| --- | --- | --- |
| $2,000 | Profit on new car sale | $700 |
| 2,000 | Profit on trade-in equity | 250 |
| 400 | Profit on amount financed | 200 |
| $4,400 | Total profit | $1,150 |

As impressive as these figures are, they are by no means outlandish. Nor are they the only benefits you'll derive from becoming an *artistic* buyer. A second, and in my estimation equally important, benefit is simply the fact that you get to win. That's right. In this day of constant "rip the consumer off" tricks, scams and pressure plays, you get to come away with the satisfied smile usually worn by the salesman!

Last but not least, you will have been given the necessary ingredients to develop an attitude of buyer's confidence—that magical state of mind that can transform the dreaded task of facing a fast-talking car salesman into a contest of wit, strategy and determination that can be relished. In short, you will become a *winning* buyer, and that quality alone is one of the most difficult for a car salesman to overcome.

To end this chapter, in style, let's introduce the "professional" car salesman in his or her full glory. Once placed into motion, the saleman goes through a sequence of events. Let's preview these selling-events in **CAR WARS**, in story fashion, as he captures a typically *unprepared* car buyer—a single woman! If you're a single man, don't feel comfortable, most unprepared car buyers, don't fare well with car salesmen. And as you continue to read through the following chapters, I ask that you keep those thoughts and one other in mind at all times. Remember, when buying a car, the moment of truth comes in a small, intimidating office/cubicle. At that moment, there will be you, a man and a contract. And this you can be sure of—no matter what he says or does, he will not be your friend nor your benefactor. He will be an artist . . .

CAR WARS

SHORT STORY

(MUSIC DOWN SLOWLY as typical STREET SOUNDS come UP—horns honking, traffic, perhaps the distant squeel of a breaking car. These FADE under the following dialogue, but remain in background.)

SALESMAN                    1

.... I see. Well, ma'am, I'm glad you came in to see us. We've got some real beauties to choose from. Ah, did you have any particular type of car in mind . . .?

7

**CONSUMER**    2

Well, . . . You know, I guess this sounds silly, but, ah, I'm really not sure! I mean, I know I want something mid-sized and not too expensive . . . . And I think as far as style goes . . .

**SALESMAN**    3
(Cutting off consumer—Footsteps in background.)

Mid-sized, huh? Ma'am, I've got a car right over here that'll fit you and your pocketbook *both* to a "T"! A real sweetheart. And you're in luck! It just went on sale this morning!

**CONSUMER**    4
. . . . How much did you say it was?

**SALESMAN** 5

Tell me this, ma'am. What did you plan on spending for a car?

**CONSUMER** 6

Oh, probably around $8,500. I guess . . . at the most! And that's including my trade-in too!

**SALESMAN** 7

That your trade-in over there?

**CONSUMER**
(Excitedly)

Uh huh. It's got an automatic transmission and air conditioning! Everything works in it, even the clock! And the interior's—

**SALESMAN** 8
(Cutting off consumer.)

Ma'am, let me ask you this. If I could get you into a brand new car like this one for, say, around $9,800—and I'll tell you like it is, that's a steal—would you trade today . . .?

**CONSUMER**

Well . . . Gee, I . . . I don't know! I mean, I'd wanted to shop around some more, and—

**SALESMAN** 9
(Again cutting off consumer.)

Sure, . . . ! Sure, shop around all you want. But take my word for it, ma'am, You're not gonna find a deal like this one anywhere. And by the time you realize that, this one'll be long gone! This baby'll sell before noon!

**CONSUMER** 10

Well, I'm, ah . . . . It really is a nice car, I guess . . . . But, you know I still think—

### SALESMAN      11

Nice!!?? Ma'am, I been in this business for eleven years now, and I'll tell you like it is—This is one of the best built cars on the road for the money, and it'll get you fantastic gas milage—Ya know, I can tell you're a woman with a good feel for bargains—

                              12

I'll tell you what, just have a seat in it, see for yourself . . . . Here we go . . . . Right there . . . . Yeah.

(We hear our shopper slide into the driver's seat and the door close.)

Great, now I'll just come around over here . . .

Ya' know, last month I toured the factory in L.A. Watched them put one of these baby's together. Honest to God, the craftsmanship that goes into one of these is . . .

### DARRELL      13

Sound familiar? As if this is one car buyer that's about to, shall we say, get taken for a ride? . . . If you're like most prople, you'll probably answer yes. Why? Because at one time or another you've probably found yourself sitting right where she is . . . being controlled and probably deceived by someone we all know and fear . . . That's right, fear . . .

### DARRELL 14

... the car salesman . In fact, his reputation is so well known you *could* say he's a kind of living legend of the lots. According to that legend he's the guy who'd cheat anyone for a fast buck, right? The patton-leather fox, with the perfectly tailored suits, diamond jewelery and a gift of gab ...

### 15

... The only guy on earth who can talk you out of your life savings and make you think—for a while, at least—he's done you a favor ...

... Face it. We all dread having to face him, and when we finally do, we're nervous, wary, always on the defensive. And if you stop and think about it, that's our first mistake, since it puts him on the *offensive*—in *control*—and there is no two ways about it, *control* is the name of his game!

### CONSUMER 16

.... But that doesn't sound right at all! A friend of mine told me it was worth at least $1,200! And I saw one just the other day in the lot over by the drug store selling for $1,395!

### SALESMAN 17

Ma'am, cars are my business! I see 'em come and go—all kinds of 'em—every day. And *believe me*, yours is worth *max*, $400 . . . .

### 18

. . . . But okay, okay! You're getting ours at a rock bottom $8,700 . . . .

### CONSUMER

But I thought—

### SALESMAN
(Cutting consumer off.)

I'll tell you what.

### 19

If I can get you five for it, are you ready to drive home in that brand new car today? . . .

**CONSUMER**     **20**

Well, I . . . But, wait a minute. Before you said—

**SALESMAN**     **21**

Let's see . . . at five for your trade-in . . . against, ah, $8,700 . . . . Okay, that's $8,200. I can swing that for you at about . . . $280 a month . . . . Oh, and the banks require 30% down . . . .

**SALESMAN**     **22**

Will that be cash or check, ma'am? . . .

### CONSUMER 23

Ah . . . Check, I guess . . . . No! I mean, wait! I don't know! 30% down?! . . . and $280 a month? . . . I think I'd better just think this whole thing over first. I mean, I'm really not—

### SALESMAN 24
(Cutting in again.)

Okay, listen, I'm gonna be totally honest with you, ma'am. See, we've got this sales contest going here—a trip to Vegas—three days, all expenses, one of those things. Ma'am, my girl is really counting on it. And as of yesterday I'm only one car— ONE CAR—from winning!

### SALESMAN 25
(Conversation DOWN.)

So, anyway, I'll tell you what I'll do. I'll get you another discount. Can you handle $275 a month? . . . . And I think I can get the boss to throw in a special five year warranty policy.

### DARRELL 26

The question is, do we as consumers have any defense against this kind of treatment? Or is the car salesman *really* as crafty and unbeatable as the legend says? . . . I feel the consumer *can* win, if you know the game plan and rules car salesmen live by.

**27**

One of the first things a woman has to do, and for that matter, *any* car buyer, is to understand exactly what they're up against when they step onto a car lot. I mean, here's Joan Smith. She's a young girl, right? She's not a salesperson, doesn't have expertise in financing, terms, interest, and she's not particularly mechanically inclined either!

**28**

Now, what she's facing is not only a salesman probably with years of experience at the art of double talk, shuffling papers, and switching figures, but a whole *regiment* of these guys! A *team*!!

## DARRELL                29

I'm not kidding. New car dealerships, used ones too, for that matter, are a lot like a fortress. The sales manager is the top dog. He's like the general. He runs the whole show— sees and okays *every* deal written on the lot. Now, he's got years of experience under his belt and he's after one thing—**Profit!**

**30**

. . . . Then there's the closers. These guys could be thought of as the general's highest ranking officers. They're the salesman's bosses. They're experienced, top notch sellers, too, and their specialty, alot of times, is taking over for the salesman . . .

**31**

Once you're in the sales booth, and the salesman has made you a bunch of vague "promises", if you want to call 'em that, in comes the closer. He'll try to take back everything the salesman "gave" and then some. Closers can really put the pressure on . . .

### DARRELL 32

And finally the front line troopers — the salesmen themselves — out there day in and day out, sellling, selling, selling — they're all pro's. They've got to be to last in the business as competitive and dynamic as retail car sales . . . . Now picture this whole bunch working together in a professional, coordinated operation with a single, all important objective . . . . .

### 33

. . . Take the *maximum* amount of dollars in exchange for each and every car sold from each and every Joan Smith and John Doe who sets foot on the lot!

The funny part, though, is this. As professional and high-powered as the sales force is, the consumer *can* beat 'em at their own game! And it's really not that complicated . . .

### 34

Actually it's a matter of being in the know. See, the salesman is a master of deception. So, if you assume or approximate *anything*, he'll convince you you're full 'o beans and he's right every time . . . .

A common example is the old, "If I could, would you?" technique. He'll dangle what we call consumer carrots in front of you and try to get you to commit yourself as a *now* buyer.

Listen, if I could get you my car at $1,000 under sticker, would you buy today?" ... Sounds great, right? Now, if you say yes, you've made a commitment and he won't let you forget it, believe me. But he hasn't committed a thing. He just said. "*If* I could" and once you're in the sales office, that closer will come in and start taking those carrots away as fast as the salesman gave them out . . . .

**36**

Planning is important, too. Once you've gotten all the facts together, you've got to sit down and put together a step-by-step plan of attack. One of the things we suggest a woman include, for instance, is what we call a third baseman . . . .

**37**

He or she is a friend or relative whose one and only job is to keep the salesman off balance. She does this by occassionally getting her "two cents" in about certain pre-planned dislikes she has about the car—

Gas millage, interior, the ride, anything. This is a continual irritation to the salesman. Besides that, it weakens his control and concentration . . . . He's trying to talk you *into* something, and she's very subtly, but firmly, trying to talk you *out* of it.

The whole point is when you go in with a plan, and you're like we said, "in the know", the salesman can't possibly deceive you. With that kind of advanced knowledge and a few buyer's techniques of your own, *you're* the one that's in control, even though the salesman doesn't know it . . . .

**39**

Sounds involved, but actually it's not. All the facts are available to all of us. It's a matter of a few phone calls, a trip to the bank and maybe the library, and some simple math . . . .

**40**

I'll put it this way—you can be fully prepared in less than a day. And when you stop to think that time can save you easily hundreds and maybe *thousands* of dollars, depending on the type of car you buy . . . . Besides that, and honest to God, this is worth as much to me as the money . . .

### DARRELL 41

You get to strip this legendary con-man of his reputation! You get to *win*!! I think that's really neat! . . .

(Long pause.)

It really boils down to one of two ways—you either prepare in advance or you can almost bet your boots they'll take you to the cleaners . . . .

### SALESMAN 42

. . . Now with tax, license, our special dealership detail package, and that five year warranty policy, that's . . . Ah, only $10,995.98 . . . Let's see . . . minus $525 for your trade-in, and . . . Oh, right, I have your down payment check for $2,000.

### 43

That leaves a balance of . . . $8,270 . . . See, by golly! We did get you in at under $8,500! How about that!

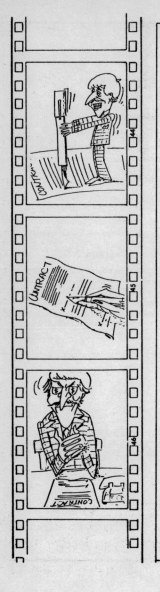

**44**

. . . And lets see, that's payable at only $285 a month for 48 months . . .

**45**

. . . Now if you'll just sign right here, here, and . . . here, before the boss changes his mind . . . .

**46**

That's right . . . Where all the "X's" are . . . Fine . . . .

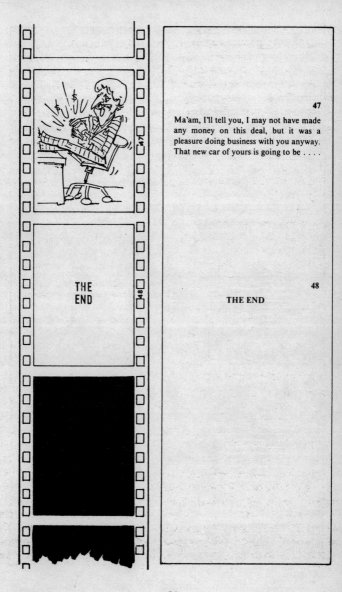

**47**

Ma'am, I'll tell you, I may not have made any money on this deal, but it was a pleasure doing business with you anyway. That new car of yours is going to be . . . .

**48**

**THE END**

# CHAPTER TWO

# DISPELLING LEGENDS

## THE TYPICAL BUYER'S
## TRUE OR FALSE CAR SALESMAN QUIZ

|  | | TRUE | FALSE |
|---|---|---|---|
| 1. | Car salesmen are dishonest cheats. | ......... | ......... |
| 2. | Car salesmen are silver-tongued, flashy dressers totally without scruples. | ......... | ......... |
| 3. | For the right price a car salesman would sell his mother into slavery. | ......... | ......... |
| 4. | The one and only thing a car salesman enjoys in life is bilking a honest, hard-working person like you out of your money. | ......... | ......... |
| 5. | All car salesmen should be imprisoned. | ......... | ......... |

Do any of these sound familiar? True? Granted most are exaggerations, but they are nonetheless common statements spoken by typical buyers who characterize the car salesman according to the image previously mentioned. And it is people attuned to this image who are *exactly* the kind a car salesman loves to see come strolling onto his lot. The reason for this is simple. He knows perfectly well buyers who view him according to his legendary image are afraid of him. That's right, afraid.

27

And what effect does this element of fear and the car salesman's knowledge that it exists, have on the bargaining process? Very simply it puts him *two* up on the typical buyer before a word is ever spoken! For not only does it place him on the offensive, at the same time it gives him the *control* that comes with that position, and this is exactly what he wants.

Step one, then, of the buyer's art is simple: **STRIP THE CAR SALESMAN OF HIS LEGENDARY ARMOR.** Take him for exactly what he is and nothing more—a normal, flesh and blood person like you; a married man with children to feed and clothe and a mortgage to pay off; a man in an extremely competitive "now you're hired, now you're fired" line of work; a person who puts in long hours, working nights and weekends, while the majority of us are barbecuing steaks or sipping drinks in front of our TV sets; in short, a person to *respect*.

Let's take a few moments to briefly define that phrase "extremely competitive, 'now you're hired, now you're fired' line of work." There are thousands of new car dealerships in the United States today. The average dealership will be manned by roughly 10 salesmen, 3 closers and 2 sales managers. In one weekend it is common for a sales force like this to sell anywhere from 20 to 30 cars. If we apply a reasonably *low* average profit figure to those cars—say $ 2,000—and do some more math, we can quickly come up with a figure of $60,000— profit only *taken* in on a single weekend.

Now, a salesman who didn't sell any cars on this particular weekend will not only be left without a cut of this money, he will also "upset" the sales manager, since the boss gets a cut of every deal written on the lot. To stay employed under these kinds of conditions, the new salesman must begin almost at once competing with his counterparts. If he hasn't begun selling cars within the first month, chances are he'll be on the street looking for another job.

In short, then, successful car salesmen are *only* those who have been willing to give their profession (their art) an enormous amount of elbow grease, determination and dedication. By thus understanding the car salesman and his plight in the very beginning, you *remove* the element of fear that makes car buying a negative or losing activity and in doing so turn the initial tables of the bargaining process in *your* favor.

In the interest of the "art," however, we are going to go a step further than simply placing the car salesman in true perspective.

Since acting is one of the many "tricks" of his trade, and since you in turn must begin to develop your *own* acting skills, we are going to let you sit back a moment and view an entire "artistic" buy from beginning to end. But first let's set the stage.

Our story will aptly be entitled "Car Wars." It will pit Andy Smith and his wife Joan against some of the worst "tricksters" in the retail car sales industry. Consider Joan and Andy two undercover soldiers fighting for an independent cause—monetary survival in an over-inflated economy. And the villains? Salesmen, of course—front line troopers. The battlefield is located at a new car dealership—the salesmen's fortress!

As our drama unfolds, keep these few points in mind. First, simply relax and "watch." Don't worry about taking notes or forgetting any of the tips you will be given. *Chapter 8* will furnish you with both a step-by-step summary and a quick and easy means of referring to specific parts of the book as they will apply to your own artistic buy. Second, try to picture *yourself* in one of the leading roles. Imagine yourself following the simple steps Joan and Andy follow in preparation for your *own* next auto purchase. With that kind of involvement, when you *do* buy your next car, you'll be a confident and fully prepared artistic buyer. And the result? You'll quickly find out those profit savings mentioned in *Chapter 1* aren't just exorbitant numbers pulled out of the imagination—they're real savings you can easily reap and take pride in yourself for having done so.

One more thing. Keep in mind also when we say "worst of the tricksters" we mean exactly that. Some dealerships are perfectly reputable and would never allow "tactics" used against buyers such as Andy and Joan will encounter. On the other hand, many are bounded only by the limits of human innovation when it comes to plotting ways in which to literally pick the typical buyer's pocket right under his or her nose. Since you stand a chance of encountering either on your next auto purchase, we've chosen to prepare you for the worst.

Obviously, then, it goes without saying, Joan and Andy's mission is a simple but extremely delicate one. They must enter the fortress and drive away in the car of *their* choice at the price of *their* choice.

Since this will be a battle without bloodshed, we can rest assured that no matter what happens they'll come away with their lives. If their mission is unsuccessful, though, it may just be a different story for their bankbooks. Now, since they're getting top billing and we as an audience would hate to get bored, let's take a moment to thicken the plot a bit by stacking the odds against them. Here's what they're facing:

The "fortress" is considered by most of their fellow buyers impenetrable. Not only is the General (the sales manager) who controls the entire operation a shrewd, seasoned and extremely determined man, he is also renowned as a strategist. Every deal written in his fortress must first get his approval, and the one thing he is looking for on every contract that crosses his desk is profit.

Surrounding him is a small but elite group of officers (Closers—the salesmen's bosses) each of whom is also a specialist in his field or the General would never allow him to help command his operation. These officers have a single, common dream—to one day wield the General's power. And each knows perfectly well that to do so, he must totally dedicate himself to the dealership's cause; prevent independent men and women like Joan and Andy from driving out of the fortress with a car purchased at a price they can live with.

As formidable as the General and his officers are, though, they are not our couple's main concern. For the moment, at least, it is the front line trooper (the Salesman) who is on their minds. That man who knows the art of selling cars inside out. The aggressive man who has dealt with buyers from all occupations and walks of life. The man who has heard every trick, excuse and hard-luck story in the book and who nonetheless consistently sells the dealership's cars at a maximum profit.

It goes without saying, our leading man and woman will have their hands full. But like any true hero or heroine, the challenge only makes them more determined. And we in the audience aren't worried a bit. Especially since as our story opens we see them acting true to form.

They have just stepped from a small boulevard deli. Andy has a copy of a local newspaper turned to the car ads section tucked under his arm. Obviously he has decided that in order to pull this mission off, both he and Joan must first arm themselves with a veritable arsenal of car buying savvy. They both stand for a long moment gazing across the boulevard at the sprawling fortress. Then, before opening the doors to their obviously tired 10-year-old trade-in, Joan suddenly smiles knowingly. "Yes," she whispers to herself, "we must first arm up!"

# CHAPTER THREE

# 3
# ARMING UP

The gathering and analysis of accurate intelligence has been
a deciding factor in most wars. The reason is obvious. The
ability to know in advance an adversary's strategy and formulate
one's own strategy accordingly carries with it an immense
advantage. In the world of retail car sales, although it is not
lives but dollars on the line, these same conditions apply. And
since Joan and Andy have decided that before entering into
a bargaining session they must first arm themselves with every
advantage possible, this intelligence gathering process will be
their first order of business.

Before they begin, however, we in the audience are going
to make several assumptions for and about our dynamic duo.
Let's assume they are a dollar-conscious and highly analytical
couple. It is because of these qualities they have *already* taken
the time to sit down and have a realistic discussion as to what
make and model of car *best* fits their needs, lifestyle and the
limits of their bank accounts. The results of that discussion
are as follows:

They've decided to buy a new car and find several of the
more popular makes attractive. As far as the model goes, a
midsized, two-door sedan seems most likely. Joan feels this
will comfortably accommodate their family and friends and not

send too many of their hard-earned dollars into the gas tank and out of the tailpipe. Since both do a good deal of stop and go freeway driving, they'll want an automatic transmission. In considering the countless extras available these days they've assumed (correctly) that they could easily add up to a substantial increase in the price of the car and, since payments on a new car alone will probably put somewhat of a cramp on their lifestyle, they'll most likely get along with as few frills as possible. A radio and heater are essential, of course, and since they live in an area which as a rule "sizzles" in the summertime, they'll almost surely require an air conditioner. That's about it for now, with the exception of the color, which at this point is a toss-up between sky blue (Joan) and cocoa brown (Andy).

Now, about that intelligence, our couple will divide it into two categories—the first called "soft" intelligence. This is information which for the most part is basic and general in nature and which can be obtained without coming in contact with the adversary. Its purpose is simply to furnish the artistic buyer with a general overview as to current new car prices and quality, along with some specific pointers in the areas of how and where to borrow money. In a nutshell, it is the basic foundation upon which Andy and Joan will later use "hard" intellience to build their buyer's plan.

And where does this *soft* intelligence come from? Well, part of it comes from the new car ads section of that newspaper we recently saw folded under Andy's arm. Cars galore! Deals galore! Prices and terms galore! Now spread in all their deceptive glory on the Smith's living room carpet. While both understand that on-the-spot ad buying is dangerous business (in most cases it leads to impulsive buying, which as we've previously mentioned leads to being taken to the cleaners) they also know the car ads carry much information which will serve to give them a general "feel" for the retail marketplace. They are a quick and easy way, for instance, of comparing the prices of various makes and models. (Keep in mind they are sale priced—usually $500 to $1,000 lower than what you will encounter on the lot.) Many also advertise financing and terms—another subject the Smith s will want to start becoming familiar with.

An hour later, after a thorough look and much discussion, Joan and Andy agree the popular makes and models offering generally what they had in mind are running in the area of $10,000. Also, they have found one advertised at "X" number of dollars down and "convenient monthly payments of only $ . . ."—which doesn't really sound too hard to handle. But Andy took the time to read the fine print in that particular ad. Camouflaged among its barely discernible words and numbers, he discovered something called the **APR** or **Annual Percentage Rate.** Following this was a percentage figure (probably in the area of 18%—"on approved credit") and in that same small print a "deferred price." In comparing the advertised sale price against the deferred price he noticed quite a sizable difference, a difference adding up to somewhere in the neighborhood of a three thousand dollar boost in the price of the car! Obviously those "convenient" terms don't come cheaply! But more about that shortly.

Since Joan had a hunch that more valuable *soft* intelligence might be found in many of the consumer and car performance magazines, late that morning the couple stopped by the library and leafed through a copy or two (**CONSUMER REPORTS, MOTOR TREND** and **CHANGING TIMES** are all excellent, by the way). In scanning their pages she and Andy found her hunch was right! Much of the information published in these periodicals deals with unbiased comparisons of actual performance tests pitting various popular makes and models against each other. As a result, in another reasonably short period of time the Smiths gained a good deal of factual insight as to the quality of the cars they had been considering. (NOTE: Another source of soft intelligence is friends or acquaintances who may have recently purchased a car similar to what you're in the market for. A word of caution here, though. Very few people, friend or foe, will admit to having been taken in a car deal or to the fact that the car they bought hasn't really performed the way they'd hoped. Your best means of extracting the information you need in this situation is simply to take all that is said with a grain of salt, ask to drive the car yourself and, coupled with any other information you may have been able to gain, come to your own conclusions.)

With a general feel for the marketplace under their belts and some insight as to how various cars perform, the Smiths choices are now beginning to narrow. At this point they begin to give a little further consideration to that $10,000. Where, for instance, is it going to come from? Like the majority of consumers, they can't afford to shell out that kind of money in cash, so they'll obviously have to borrow it. But from whom and on what terms? The initial answers to these questions (they will undoubtedly go through a few changes in the process of developing a buyer's plan) are particularly valuable bits of *soft* intelligence.

But, rather than starting from scratch as complete novices and going through all of the usual complex and time consuming steps involved in educating themselves on financing and terms, let's take a moment to become familiar with a few simple, time saving steps they are *already* familiar with.

They know, for instance, that although interest rates can be, and traditionally *are*, quoted in countless confusing and misleading ways, the **APR** in that car ad which caught Andy's eye is the one simple figure they need be concerned with since it tells them the *true* interest rate they'll be paying on the money they borrow. In addition, they know that the longer the time frame in which they borrow the money, the *lower* their monthly payments will be, but the *higher* that **APR** will be. In short, the longer the loan the more of a convenience for them and the more of a risk to the lender, thus the more expensive it is. Dollar-and-cents wise, then, the simplest and quickest way to find out which lender is offering the most economical loan deal is simply to ask each for the **APR** and total dollar payback (the "deferred price") and then compare. The lowest figures are the cheapest loan.

To help clarify this, the Smiths are now about to put their knowledge to work by doing exactly what any artistic buyer would do in order to find his or her most economical lender.

They are first going to erase at once any temptation that may exist in their minds to borrow the money from a "quick and easy" loan company unless absolutely necessary! Here's why: Loan companies will usually charge the highest interest rates around. In addition, most make "personal" rather than car loans and thus require collateral in the form of everything from your bedroom set to the second trust deed on your house. Also included in their "quick and easy" deals are such things as prepayment penalties, balloon payments, escrow fees and exorbitant commission fees.

So what are the Smiths and your choices? Dealerships, banks (preferably your own bank) and credit unions.

First, let's take a moment to consider dealerships. As a rule they will be the most expensive of the three mentioned. Don't totally discount them, though, since there are ways (which the Smiths will show us) to use dealership financing to your advantage. For now simply keep in mind that dealerships don't make loans themselves; they borrow the money from their own banks or loan institutions. And every contract they write for that institution yields them (the dealership) a percentage profit. This is accomplished simply by charging *you* a higher interest rate than they pay out. This means the convenient "14% on approved credit" Andy saw advertised in the paper can, and often does, become 18% at the drop of a hat!

With this in mind the Smiths are simply going to consider the dealership as a possible option and concentrate, for the moment, on the other two choices. With a pencil, paper and pocket calculator before her, Joan is in the process of making a few calls.

The first is to her bank. She has asked to speak to the loan arranger and told him that she and Andy have an account with them and they are shopping around for a car loan. They are planning, she says, on a new car and will probably want to borrow somewhere in the neighborhood of $8,000 (A $2,000 downpayment is being planned). All they're interested in at the moment are the terms available time-wise, the annual percentage rate and total dollar payback on each of these terms, and what each would work out in monthly payments.

The loan arranger then tells Joan something like this: Since she *does* bank with them, the **APR** will be a "preferred" or lower rate than that given to just anyone. The money is available on a number of timetables up to (probably) 60 months, but the most popular choices are usually 36 or 48 months. After a bit of figuring he continues by saying that on a 36 month loan the **APR** would be 13.5% and the total dollar payback would be $9,773 at $271 per month. On 48 months, the APR would be 14%. The total dollar payback on this would be $ 10,493 at $218 per month. He asks that she keep in mind, however, the maximum they will loan is 80% (this figure may vary) of the new car "sticker" or suggested retail price, plus tax and license. And being a very efficient loan arranger he doesn't even drop the conversation here. He also asks whether Joan will be trading in her present car. When she tells him the year, make and model, the number of miles it's been driven, and any extras she may have on it, he will check his *Bluebook, Redbook* or *Brownbook* listing and tell her what her car is worth. She gives him this information and a few moments later finds out her trade-in has a wholesale value of $2,000, minus any repairs it may require. She then thanks him and after thinking that one over for a moment, decides to ask him one more question. Can he also tell her the wholesale value of *new* cars? Indeed he can. Again, she tells him the vital statistics— make, model, extras and so forth, and shortly thereafter finds out that the *wholesale* value of one of the cars they're considering is $8,500.

Joan's second call is to her credit union and she asks the same questions: **APR,** terms, total dollar payback and monthly payments. Credit union figures are a bit different, though. On a 36 month loan, the **APR** is 10.12% for a total dollar payback of $9,499. Monthly that's $263. At 48 months: **APR** 10.5%. Total dollar payback $9,824, payable at $204 per month. Again, though, the maximum is 80% of the sticker price plus tax and license, and the same *Bluebook* listings are available.

Now a quick comparison of **APR's** and total dollar paybacks tells the Smiths that for the moment the credit union is their cheapest lender. At this point they could make calls to other banks, but chances of beating a credit union's terms are slim. Besides, there's something else on their minds now. Andy feels a 20% down payment may create a bit of a problem for their savings goals but a little simple math negates his suspicions.

$10,000   Approximate selling price without the $2,000
          (ADMS) [1]
 2,000    Smith's wholesale value on trade-in
_____
 $8,000   Difference in price

[1]   *Dealership is using an Additional Dealer Markup Sticker (ADMS) to
      capture additional profits. These "Stickers" start off with siding, trim,
      undercoating, fabric guard, polyguard, special wheels and tires and end
      with extra profit for hard to get automobiles.*

This leaves Andy and Joan owing a bottom-line figure of
around $8,000. + tax & licence, if the salesman would hold
true to this negotiating offer. If the Smiths actually captured
this car for $10,000, 80% financing with any load company
could be easily secured, and no downpayment,—in cash
required. [2] Unfortunately, the dealership will offer less for the
trade-in and some downpayment will be required. Therefore,
the Smiths have one of three choices: look for a cheaper car,
try to secure a personal rather than a car loan— for which
they'll probably have to give an arm and a leg in collateral,
commission fees, interest, and so on or depending on how
creative and determined they are, raise the money in some other
way.

For purposes of **Car Wars** they have the money but, as
we've mentioned, they're also an extremely savings minded
couple. In looking at the figures before them, the writing on
the wall is fast becoming clear. The *higher* the trade-in price
they can get for their car and the *lower* the selling price on
the new car, the less down payment they'll have to withdraw
from those savings—and the less they will have to pay out
monthly.

Just as we might have expected, it is now an even greater
sense of determination we suddenly see in them, and for good
reason. With a minimum of time and effort they have laid the
foundation. In doing so, they have further strengthened their
position as artistic buyers and at the same time completed the
first half of step two of the buyer's art: **KNOW THE
MARKETPLACE.** And as this scene closes, we applaud them—
for the confident manner in which Andy snatches up the car

keys and they both head for the door—on their way to meet the adversary.

*2   *Please remember this $10,000 figure has a built-in profit margin of around 15%, $1,500, and that dealerships may add an ADMS for further profit-taking in the marketplace.*

# CHAPTER FOUR

# HARD INTELLIGENCE

**EIGHT BUYER'S COMMANDMENTS**

1. I WILL VISIT A MINIMUM OF THREE DEALERSHIPS.

2. I WILL MAKE EVERY EFFORT TO CONTACT AND DEAL WITH A YOUNG SALESMAN.

3. I WILL REMAIN AT ALL TIMES AWARE OF THE SALESMAN'S GOALS AND THE WAYS HE WILL ATTEMPT TO CONTROL ME INTO ACHIEVING THEM.

4. I WILL CONTROL THE SALESMAN *MYSELF* WITH LOOKER/BUYER VACILLATION.

5. I WILL TAKE THE CARD OF EACH SALESMAN I DEAL WITH AND NOTE ON IT THE CAR OF MY INTEREST, INCLUDING ITS ASKING PRICE AND ANY "OFFERS" THE SALESMAN HAS MADE ME.

6. I WILL TEST DRIVE ONLY THE CARS I AM CONSIDERING OR IDENTICAL LOT CARS.

7. **AVIOD ANY SERIOUS NEGOTIATING EFFORTS OUTSIDE ON THE DEALERSHIP'S CAR LOT. MAKE NO OFFERS AT THIS TIME.**

8. **UNDER NO CIRCUMSTANCES WILL I ENTER A SALESMAN'S OFFICE DURING THIS PHASE OF MY MISSION.**

With the foundation for their buyer's plan firmly established, Andy and Joan must now gather the raw materials for the plan itself—*hard* intelligence. What this means in specifics: *The* car they will buy, for instance, and its *wholesale* and *retail* price. The *dealership* and the *salesman* they will bargain with. That salesman's *selling-techniques* and their *buying techniques* for countering and controlling the bargaining process.

To get this kind of intelligence they will obviously have to enter the fortress, meet the adversary face-to-face and begin to match wits. While this may sound fairly simple, it is actually a very delicate part of their mission. Remember, they'll now be dealing first hand with professionals in the art of persuasion—men whose single most important goal is to get typical buyers into a salesman's office and go to work on their bank account.

It is precisely because of this "delicacy" that the above-mentioned **Buyer's Commandments** are of prime importance. With this in mind, while the Smiths are on the road to their first dealership, let's take time out to examine each in detail and see exactly how they apply.

## 1. I WILL VISIT A MINIMUM OF THREE DEALERSHIPS.

An artistic buyer's first commandment is nothing more than good old shopper's horse sense. It is a bargain you're after, right? Well, a car is like any other product for sale in the retail marketplace. The same make and model may vary anywhere from a few dollars to over a thousand, depending on where you shop and what options you decide to include. Note the word "minimum" in this rule, also. With a pretty firm idea already in mind as to the car you want, you will most likely be able to find it at a decent starting price on one of three lots. If not, though, you may have to shop around a bit more.

In any case a single morning or afternoon should allow you ample time.

## 2. I WILL MAKE EVERY EFFORT TO CONTACT AND DEAL WITH A YOUNG SALESMAN.

As was previously mentioned, turnover in the car selling profession is high. Because of this, a young salesman is very likely to be a *new* salesman, which is exactly what you want. Here's why. Being new in the business, he will lack the hardened "take 'em to the cleaners at all cost" attitude of the more experienced veteran. Along the same lines, his persuasive skills will probably not be fully developed. And finally, remember, he is keenly aware that in order to remain employed he must sell cars. In order to accomplish this and gain an initial foothold in the profession, there's a good chance he'll work his heart out for you and settle for a sale "on the books" even if the commission is small. If not, the "General" himself may see some future promise in this young car salesman and close **YOUR DEAL** for little profit, showing a sale on the books, to encourage this salesman to stay with them.

## 3. I WILL REMAIN AWARE OF THE SALESMAN'S GOAL AT ALL TIMES AND THE WAYS IN WHICH HE WILL ATTEMPT TO CONTROL ME INTO ACHIEVING THEM.

What exactly are the salesman's goals? Well, obviously his ultimate or long range goal is to sell you a maximum profit car for a maximum amount of dollars. In the beginning, though, he has a few very critical short range goals to take care of. The first is to accurately size you up and immediately place you into one of an assortment of "typical" buyer categories. Are you a real buyer at all, for instance—a person who if handled properly will buy today—or just a "looker"—a person who passes the day going from lot to lot with no intention of really spending a dime? Are you "typically" nervous, impulsive, gullible? Or do you come off as an aggressive "tough customer" type? Are you informed or "typically" uninformed as to car prices and terms? If he is able to place you into the category of a real buyer and a "typically uninformed" one, he will feel very comfortably in control and immediately go to work manipulating you into achieving his second short range goal—making you commit yourself verbally to the fact that "yes" you will buy today. With one and two out of the way, he will quickly move to number three—to some way, **ANY WAY UNDER THE SUN,** get you into his office where he or a closer can really go to work on you.

## 4. I WILL CONTROL THE SALESMAN MYSELF WITH LOOKER/BUYER VACILLATION.

What exactly does vacillation mean? To waver with indecision. To change both your mind and also your "typical buyer's category" at the proper times, in order to keep him (the salesman) off base. It's your means of *not* letting the salesman achieve any of the above-mentioned goals. As an example, for the most part you must come off very business-like and unemotional. Occasionally, though, drop in a "typically uninformed" statement or two to give him second thoughts. And while you will not commit yourself as a "yes buyer" today, you will imply it's definitely a possibility. The results? Confusion on the salesman's part and *control* on yours!

## 5. I WILL TAKE THE CARD OF EACH SALESMAN I DEAL WITH AND NOTE ON IT THE CAR OF MY INTEREST, INCLUDING ITS ASKING PRICE AND ANY "OFFERS" THE SALESMAN HAS MADE ME.

Again, good old horse sense. The cards you gather will later serve as reminders and reference material when developing your buyer's plan. In addition, even though the "promises" the salesman has made are, in all probability, "questionable," if recorded, they can be used as leverage for a starting point with whatever salesman you do decide to buy from.

## 6. I WILL TEST DRIVE ONLY THE CARS I AM CONSIDERING OR IDENTICAL LOT CARS. IN NO CASE WILL I TEST DRIVE A "DEMO."

Pay particular attention to this commandment with these points in mind. You *cannot* accurately judge a car's performance by driving an identical dealership demo. If a dealer insists that you do (and some will), take your business elsewhere. Here's the reason. Demos can, and often will, have been given high performance tuning in order to be specially prepared for "typically easy buyers." The factory-delivered car you end up with may not perform nearly as well. To play it safe, insist on driving *the* car you are considering or an identical lot car. A demo can be recognized by the license plate. It will have the word "Dealer" stamped on the plate itself.

## 7. AVIOD ANY SERIOUS NEGOTIATING EFFORTS OUTSIDE ON THE DEALERSHIP'S CAR LOT. MAKE NO OFFERS AT THIS TIME.

The saleman's objective is to sell you a maximum profit car **TODAY!** He will begin to negotiate almost instantly on the lot. "Make me an offer!" he'll say. I suggest you return to the special task of locating the "right" car. The salesman's mission is to *entice* you to begin dealing outside the salesman's office. The "real" dealing occurs inside the salesman's office *always*. Meanwhile, the salesman gains some insight as to your negotiating abilities and weaknesses out on the car lot. Not a good position for any car buyer.

## 8. I WILL, UNDER *NO* CIRCUMSTANCES, ENTER A SALESMAN'S OFFICE DURING THIS PHASE OF MY MISSION.

This, in some cases, is easier said than done. I repeat— you are dealing with shrewd professional people. Persuasiveness, and in some cases, high pressure tactics, are an every day part of their occupation. Keep the following little truism in mind and you should have no problem: **ANYTHING AND EVERYTHING** a car salesman says before getting you into his office is, as I've said is "questionable." In most cases his promises are nothing more than disappearing consumer "carrots" dangled in front of you with one intent and one intent only in mind to lead you into his office. Once there, the carrots will quickly begin to disappear and the high pressure will begin to get poured on as the **REAL DEAL** begins to emerge.

So much for definitions. Since the Smiths are just pulling up front of that first dealership, it seems we're just in time to let them now *show* us how these work on the "man" himself.

The lot is a huge, glistening expanse, centered by a massive showroom and adjoining offices. The "troopers" are out in full force. There is an older, chubby one milling about at the showroom entrance, a few inside and several chatting among the rows of cars. Then, suddenly, Andy spies what they're after— a young one, fairly handsome and, of course, well-groomed. He is stepping from one of the offices, looking in need of a buyer. The Smiths quickly exit their car, take a deep breath, and move onto the lot in the direction he is walking. (A note of caution. Since salesmen, like predators, often have their own "territorial" portions of a lot, you may have to do a bit of dodging and weaving in order to cross their turfs and get to the one you want. If you happen to be approached before you reach him, simply say, "Thank you, but I'd like to speak to the other gentleman over there." Oh, and don't stop walking while you say it!) As they approach, he smiles, probably already sizing them up as a "typical" well-to-do family.

"Hi, I'm Jay Wilson," he says cordially. "Can I help you?"

"Yes. I'm Andy Smith. This is my wife Joan. We're shopping for a new car."

"Well, Andy and Joan, I've got some great cars and *fantastic* deals! Did you have anything in particular in mind?"

"Yes, we do," Joan says, "we're looking for a mid-sized car, a two door, and probably with air conditioning."

"I think I've got one right over here you might be interested in. This one is one of our hottest sellers right now. In fact, I think this is the only one we've got left."

"Very attractive," Andy says. "It, ah, looks a bit rich for our blood, though. Mag wheels, electric windows, racing stripes ... how much is it?"

"This one is $12,600. And I'll be perfectly honest with you, that's a buy. These babies are really in demand. By next year this car will be worth $14,000 easy, the way they're appreciating."

"No," Andy continues, peeking in at the red velour upholstery and electric sun roof. "That's out of our range. We really don't want all that extra stuff anyway." While saying this he catches a look at the manufacturer's sticker. The suggested retail price says $10,200. "Why the difference in your price?," Andy spouts.

But Mr. Wilson seems to have ignored his statement. "Are you trading a car, folks?"

"Yes, we are," Joan says. "That's ours right over there."

"And how much did you plan on spending?"

"Probably not over $10,000."

"Well, we're really not too far off base, then. I think we can get you into something like this for not too much more than that."

"Well, actually, what we had in mind was $10,000, less what we get for our trade-in."

"I see. And what do you feel your car is worth?"

"Well, gee, I'm really not sure . . . . Ah . . . ."

Up to this point Andy and Joan have been fairly businesslike. And Wilson, of course, has been trying to size them up. He probably had them placed into the category of semi-tough customers until this last little statement of Joan's. Hesitation and not knowing the value of your own car is much more "typically uninformed"—much more comfortable for him to use to start taking control. Now he looks Joan straight in the eye.

"Let me ask you this. If I could get you $3,000 (highball offer) for your trade-in and talk, oh, around $10,000 (lowball offer) for this car—and that's a steal, believe me—would you be interested in driving it home today?"

Now, another "typical" move on Andy's part *infers* rather than commits them both to being possible "yes" buyers today. He smiles, hesitates again and says to Joan, "You know, it really is a nice car . . . ."

Wilson's feeling more comfortable and confident all the time. Since Andy and Joan have accomplished what they wanted, though, vacillated into a new buyer "category" and inferred they *may* just buy today, it's time to pull the rug out from under him. Before he can start dangling more of those carrots, they stop hesitating, do away with the uncertain smiles, and suddenly become totally decisive.

"No. This isn't the car we want," Andy says. "We don't care for all those extras. Besides, all this pinstriping and that red velour turns me off. How about you, hon?"

"I agree," answers Joan.

51

"Do you have anything with just a radio, heater and air? Something in blue or cocoa brown?"

This has hit Wilson from left field. While he's recovering— trying to reestablish exactly what kind of buyers these two are, he stalls. "Well, now . . . let me see . . . ."

Suddenly, Andy spies a sleek mid-sized, two-door sedan— the make and model they had in mind—and in cocoa brown at that! Starting toward it he continues, "Something like that one. Over there."

"Yeah," Wilson spouts, hurrying to catch up with the couple. 'That's a nice little car! A real gem!" While walking toward the car he decides if he's going to take control he's got to find out more about this pair. "Do you work in the area, Mr. Smith?" he asks politely.

Andy decides to make him work a little harder for what he wants, which of course, is to find out if Andy has a job and if it's the kind that pays the *money* he'll need to buy today.

"Yes, I do."

"Let me guess. You're both in real estate?"

"No, actually we both are engineers at a local aircraft company."

"Oh . . . . What type engineers are you?"

"Design Engineers."

"Professionals . . ."

"Right."

The Smiths have now answered a question for Wilson and also posed him a challenge. They *definitely* have the money to buy today and may well be *tough* customers after all!

And now he's going to answer one for them. Since the subject is professions, Joan feels this is an ideal time to see if she can find out whether he's a new salesman or not. She continues immediately, but now (vacillates again) with a pleasant smile. "You look young to be a car salesman. Have you been in the business long?"

"Actually, no," he says. "I've only been here a few months. In fact, I'm trying to get established now, which is another reason I'll fix you up with a good deal. I need to get few sales under my belt."

Perfect, she thinks, *provided* that wasn't just another "carrot" (which it very well could be).

They've arrived at the car in question and both like it. And, even more attractive is the sticker price—$10,000! Not letting on how attractive the car is to them, Andy asks dryly, "How much is this one?"

"I'll tell you. We should get $12,000 for it, but if you feel it might be the car you want to buy today, I'll do better than that for you. No air in this one, though." He swings open the door.

The Smiths are in no rush to get in, though. "Why $12,000 in the first place?" Andy asks looking him straight in the eye. "The sticker price says $10,000."

Since this is a fairly common question, Wilson has a stock bit of double-talk all ready. "That sticker price means nothing. That's straight off the line at the factory. By the time we get the car here, get it detailed, inspected and totally checked out we've got hundreds in it easy. In fact, more. Folks, all our cars go through a strict systematic dealer prep. with highly trained people, before the manager will let us pull them out front. I'll tell you, the guy insists on running a really quality and customer satisfaction oriented operation. Besides these cars are in high demand in this area. **THE BOSS** demands top dollar to sell them! Special wheels and tires, trim and undercoating protect your investment. The value in these cars lasts a lifetime.

While there's some truth in what he's just said, most of this little spiel is, shall we say, typically overstated. First, the suggested retail price is exactly that, a suggested price the car should sell for, which *includes* approximately a 20% profit for the dealership. And our salesman's "strict systematic dealer prep." could probably more accurately be called a half-hour spot check. And his "trained employee"? Most likely minimum skilled garage help getting minimum wage. Obviously, the **BOSS** wants to make more profit with the cars he has possession of, and is having difficulty "hiding" these extra profits. No point in showing too much of what the Smiths know at this stage of the game, though. That will come at the proper time. "Hmm... I see," Andy says, sliding into the driver's seat.

Grasping the steering wheel, gazing at the ultra-modern dash, just the *smell* of the deliciously new interior makes him like the car even more. He knows, however, this emotional involvement is exactly why Wilson asked him to sit in the car— to excite his senses, cloud his logic, make Andy think *impulsively*, thereby again putting himself in control! But instead of falling for this tactic, Andy does control himself, remembering that a car is nothing more than an *object* and there are hundreds exactly like this one on lots throughout the city. Again, he responds dryly, "Nice, but I'm not sure we'd like it without air."

"No problem," your salesman responds, "we'll get air put in it for you."

"And what will that cost us?" Joan asks.

"Let me ask you this," he says, getting ready to try again for a commitment, "do you feel that, with air and a price you can afford, this is a car you'd like to drive home today?"

Both Smiths hesitate.

He senses they are on the verge of saying yes. Actually, they're waiting to see exactly what kind and how much of a carrot he'll dangle this time.

"I'll tell you what, Mr. and Mrs. Smith. Let's take a ride in it. Then if you feel it's a car you'd like to own I'll see if I can get that air thrown in at half price. And I think I can get you a few hundred off the asking price. Could you buy at around $11,000? Today?"

But the Smiths are not about to make the commitment. They simply ignore his question (silence can be powerful) and Joan says, "I think I *would* like to drive this one."

On the test ride he is still trying to establish a foothold of control. He points out all the "exclusive" features, stresses the fact that a car like this can't *possibly* last another day on the lot. They're selling like mad, appreciating beyond belief, in popular demand, and so on. He also has a stab or two at the Smiths ego, mentioning how the car seems to fit our couple to a tee!

They don't bother to say much during all this for several reasons. First, they're intent on finding out if the car really does seem to have the quality they've read about in consumer and car magazines. Second, could it really be *the* car for them? And finally, they're maintaining a critical business-like attitude. With this last point in mind, Joan decides to counter what the salesman is saying by throwing in a few of her *dislikes* about the car. When she suddenly realizes she doesn't have any, she decides to get a bit creative. The point, remember, is to keep him off balance. In the middle of one of his spiels she stops him matter-of-factly with, "Are there other kinds of upholstery we could get if we wanted it?"

When he works his way around that one (Joan is careful not to corner him—yet), she mentions that it seems to steer a bit rough. By this time they're returning to the lot and both realize Wilson will probably go all out now with a play to get them into his office. They pull back in, park, and he does exactly as they had expected.

"I'm going to tell you like it is, folks. This car is right for you two. Perfect! And with the Saturday buyers here tomorrow it'll be gone in a matter of hours. No kidding, if you wait you'll lose it. Let me have a look at your trade-in, then we'll go into my office and write you up a deal that will be the frosting on the cake." With this he starts off in the direction of the Smiths car, *again* in an attempt to gain control by getting Joan and Andy to follow before they have a chance to think much about it.

But they don't start walking. Instead Andy says, "I'll be honest with you! We both like the car, but we'd like to do a bit more shopping. Do you have a card?" Wilson's jaw drops for a moment and Joan imagines the four letter words racing through his head. New or not, though, he's a professional. He quickly regains his composure and assures Andy and Joan they are making a terrible mistake, to which Andy responds that this may be the case, but nonetheless they are the type who like to shop before deciding. Eventually, he forks over his card and with a pair of "typical" smiles Joan and Andy bid him good day.

Immediately after getting back in their own car, Joan makes a few notes on the back of his card: "Sticker—$12,000. Offer— Air, half price and $200 off asking price, $11,000 and indicates can get $3,000 for trade-in. Make, model, extras." Then a quick glance at her watch tells her it's all taken place in a matter of only half an hour which means they have plenty of time to visit a few more lots before lunch. After all—when they're hot, they're hot!

At the second one they are unable to find a young salesman. After wandering among the cars for a few minutes trying to avoid those who look like the old pros, and waiting for a young one to appear, they finally get approached.

His name is Ben, he says in a smooth, friendly voice, and he looks like anything but a novice. He's in his mid-forties, distinctively graying at the temples, with strikingly commanding features. His gold and diamond tie clasp glistens in the sun, as do his patent leather shoes. His suit, and for that matter his entire personal appearance, is impeccable. This one they figure for a closer—maybe even the "General" himself.

As he walks them around the lot, all three chat comfortably. And, oddly enough, he does seem sincere! In fact, he seems more interested in chatting than selling cars. When they mention they are engineers he's delighted! He compliments both on their success and mentions how few couples have the intelligence and fortitude to achieve such an accomplishment. As it turns out, in fact, he had wanted to be an engineer himself as a youngster, but just didn't have the kind of determination they had—the reason why he has ended up selling cars for the past 20 years.

Eventually, they find themselves standing before a sleek piece of machinery, sticker priced at $12,900. As Ben frankly points out, though, (he's calling both by their first names, incidentally) they can shop and shop, and what it all boils down to is the simple fact that quality—true perfection—costs a bit more. But it's worth it. And, of course, it's obvious the Smiths are an above average couple, and one way or the other they'll end up with a quality car. They honestly don't seem like the type to accept anything less. Of course, if it is something cheaper they'd like to see . . .

Then Joan is behind the wheel, cruising down the boulevard and Andy and Ben are chatting about one of his more interesting physics problems. Ben is fascinated by Andy's work and by him as a person. And he has turned the air conditioning on and the car drives like a dream, and the stereo is quietly blending an exquisite concert with the smell and feel of mechanical perfection . . .

"Andy," he says, letting them back out on the lot. "I want to be frank with you and Joan, and I don't want you to think I'm boasting—honestly. I'm the assistant manager here and I've gotten there the same way you two have gotten where you are—with a lot of plain old hard work. In my business, though, the work isn't selling innocent pleas, it's selling cars. And the reason I sell them is because I've always made it a point to sell the *right* car to the *right* person at the *right price*. I've seen too many crooked salesmen come and go in this business, believe me. The people I sell come back. They come back because they know darn well they're getting treated *right*. Now I really think this car fits you. In fact, I know it does. So here's what we'll do. I'll talk to John—he's the Manager, and I'll try to do this for you. In fact, I won't try. He'll give the okay or I won't let him use my beach house anymore! Ha! I'll get you somewhere in the ballpark of $2,000 for your trade-in and take $900 off the sticker price on this one. We'll make it an even $12,000, with say $2,000 for yours; that puts you in the car for right around $10,000—C'mon, let's get him on the phone right now . . . ."

Joan and Andy are now seated in Ben's office. He picks up the phone to dial the Manager. Suddenly he pauses for a moment and smiles. "Listen, folks, I've got to level with you on one more thing. I do have one ulterior motive in this. I'm within one car—**your car**— of making the alltime quarterly sales high for the dealership and I've got to tell you it's worth a paid week for me and my family in Mazatlan. That's another reason you're getting a below wholesale deal . . . ."

He dials and evidently gets the operator. "Jeannie, get me John, will you. Tell him I've got to talk to him about (he winks at Joan) a trip to Mexico—and tell him—huh? Well, where'd he go?" Now Ben smiles confidently—"Okay, well did he leave me holding down the fort? Anderson? You gotta be kidding! . . . Ah . . . No, I'll come up and see him myself."

Hanging up the phone, Ben suddenly looks troubled. "Listen, John's gotten off on one of his little tangents. He flies a lot and once in a while just kind of 'takes off' on the spot, if you know what I mean. He's left a guy in charge who's, well, I'll be honest with you, he's a jerk and he doesn't really care to see me get this trip. He and I don't see eye to eye, but let's write it up and I'll see if I can get it by him."

"Okay, let's see. . . . Man, he'll never buy that trade-in at that price. I know, let's bring it within reason and maybe we can make it up somewhere else in the deal. Let's see, $700; and our car was, let's see, we said an even $12,000, right . . . Okay, now dealer prep. is $350, deluxe wheels, that's . . . ahh, $280. And there's . . ."

And suddenly it dawns on Joan and Andy at the same instant. There is no John! The call was a conversation on a dead line or with another chuckling salesman! There is probably no contest, no Mexican trip, and most of all, *no* people who return to deal with Ben because he's what's known in the business as a Supersalesman! And they have just found out (nearly at the cost of their mission and the demise of their bank account) exactly what that means.

"Damn!" Andy says under his breath.

"Pardon me, Andy?"

"Ah, nothing . . . nothing," Andy says as he and Joan get to their feet and start toward the door. "Ah, Ben . . ."

"Yes, Andy?"

"Have a good trip."

By the time they finish test driving two more cars on lot number three and stop in at a fourth on their way home, the pattern has repeated itself enough times to become perfectly clear. They enter a lot and the salesman approaches. While being very courteous and polite he begins to size them up. Using the lot to try and steer them toward the more expensive models, he looks for weakness, points of leverage with which to take control. If he senses they are possible buyers, the repetitive, ever familiar "If I could . . . would *you* buy today" pitches begin. And what they all really boil down to are consumer "carrots" dangled ever so temptingly in an attempt to prime the couple for the test ride and immediate trip to the sales office. Ah, yes, and the test rides—more "promises," play at their egos, tactful "threats" that such buys can't *possibly* last another day on the lot . . . . In short, Joan and Andy now realize that from the time they step onto any car lot until the time they leave, they stand a chance of being promised anything. I repeat, **ANYTHING UNDER THE SUN** in order to be hurried through the test ride and into the salesman's office. Why? Because it is in his office—the small, intimidating cubicle—that the "carrots" vanish, promises somehow seem to simply disappear. And in their place? . . . the **REAL DEAL** begins to emerge!

# CHAPTER FIVE

# 5
# THE PLAN

So far, so good. In fact, so far excellent! Step two of the car buyer's art—**KNOW THE MARKET PLACE**—is now complete. What's more it has taken our couple the equivalent of only about one day.

Now, before actually going back to buy the car of their choice, it's back to the drawing board one last time. Why? To complete that all important third step—**HAVE A PLAN!** This means they must now take all of the intelligence gathered in their short but intense car buyer's education and from it devise the strategy that will allow them to beat the adversary at his own game.

We can break this planning segment of the Smiths mission in to three general areas. First, they must decide on the car they will buy. Second, they must come up with an *exact* dollar sum they will pay for that car, and decide on *how* they will pay for it. And finally they must understand and be prepared to bring into play a number of new **BUYER'S COMMANDMENTS** pertaining specifically to bargaining action *inside* the salesman's office.

But first things first. For purposes of our drama we are going to assume that after considering all of the pluses and minuses, Andy and Joan decided the $10,000, two-door of Mr. Jay Wilson's is the car for them. The only two problems they

63

could find with the car was it had a dealer's additional markup sticker (ADMS) for $2,000 above the full price—a bounty sticker they would deal with later in the deal. And that the car lacked air conditioning. And since they have also come to the conclusion that air is a must, the fact the dealership can have it installed for them should take care of that. In fact, looking back over their collection of salesmen's cards, they find Mr. Wilson made an offer of half price for that air. Actually getting it at that price is another thing, of course, but at least it offers a point of leverage which the Smiths will most definitely put to use.

Now for a bit of math. In a nutshell it involves taking into account every dollar applicable to the deal and from it formulating a set of fair, but "excellent buy" figures to base their strategy on. These figures can be broken down into three categories: The new car price *they will pay*, the value of their trade-in *they will demand* and the down payment.

As we know, the suggested retail price of the car the Smiths plan to purchase is $10,000. Remember, though, this figure represents what the car should sell to the public for, in order to furnish the dealership with a healthy profit—of around 20%.*³ What the Smith's are interested in, however, is not the retail, but the *wholesale* price of the car. A call to their credit union tells Andy that figure is $8,600. While he's at it Andy also asks about the price tag on the air conditioning. He's told it runs $800 retail and $595 wholesale. Since it was offered at half the retail price, the Smith's figure it in exactly that way. Now with these figures in hand and a bit of simple addition they come up with what's called the **WHOLESALE SUBTOTAL**.

| | |
|---|---|
| $8,600 | Wholesale price of car |
| + 400 | Air—retail @ half price |
| $9,000 | Wholesale subtotal (0-profit) |

---

*³   Includes a dealer bonus to be paid (3-4% of this figure) by manufacturer for selling this car.

This amount gives the couple a very close approximation of what that new car of theirs cost the dealership. Actually, it's a bit low since they figured the air at half retail ($400) instead of the $595 wholesale price.

And this brings us to their next bit of math—the inclusion of profit. Since it is a *fair* deal we're after, and since a dealership would hardly let a car go at a zero profit figure or below, this is a must. That standard 20%, though, is a bit lucrative, so the Smiths are going to trim it down a bit. In fact, they'll trim it by about 3/4th. This means instead of the normal $ 2,400 profit the dealership would expect to get, they are going to get only $500—or about 5%. Keep in mind this amount should be flexible, increasing or decreasing relative to the price of the car you are purchasing. If it's a very expensive one for instance, figure 7 to 9% profit for the dealership. On the other hand, if it's a bottom of the line make and model, make it 3 or 5%. But let's now take the $500 figure the Smiths arrived at and add it to the **WHOLESALE SUBTOTAL**.

| | |
|---|---|
| $9,000 | Wholesale subtotal |
| + 500 | 5% Profit for dealership |
| $9,500 | Selling price, including profit |

This, then, is the selling price they will bargain for as compared to the dealership's $12,600 asking price.

Ah, but unfortunately this is still not the bottom line. There's one more set of numbers neither the Smiths nor the dealership have a choice about and that's Uncle Sam's share of the action—tax and license. In California sales tax is 6%, which, based on the $9,500 total amounts to $570. The cost to license the car for the first year is available with a call to the Smith's local motor vehicles department. In their case let's say $430 the two figures combined total $1,000. Again a bit of addition:

| | |
|---|---|
| $9,500 | Selling price, including profit |
| + 1,000 | Tax and license |
| $10,500 | Bottom line price the Smiths will pay |

Joan and Andy now have an unquestionably excellent price on the car they intend to purchase. The dealership's price by this time would be in the $14,000+ range!

Now for the next category—the value (or equity) of their trade-in. This is also figured from a wholesale base. As you recall, it was quoted to you from **BLUEBOOK** as $2,000 minus any repairs it may have needed. And since we are being fair about all this, and since there is that little dent in the front fender, the Smiths are going to reduce what they will ask for it by $ 100—the approximate price of the repair. The value of their trade-in then is $1,900, at least for the moment.

Category number three is down payment, and it's here our couple has decided to change their approach a bit. In considering the figures quoted to them by the credit union, they've reasoned that payments in the $300+ range are simply too steep to handle. In order to make them more affordable without extending the loan to 48 months or more, they've decided to offer somewhere in the neighborhood of $ 1,500 down. Before deciding for sure, however, they'll discuss this with the credit union and see exactly how much it will affect those payments.

In order to see what effect this down payment and their trade-in equity will have on their deal, though, let's now go to a little subtraction:

| | |
|---|---|
| $10,500 | Bottom line purchase price |
| – 1,500 | Down payment |
| $9,000 | Bottom line price less down payment |
| – 1,900 | Trade-in equity on the Smith's car |
| $7,100 | Total money they must borrow |

As you'll recall, both the bank and credit union stipulated a maximum loan amount of 80% of the new car suggested retail price plus tax and license. This figure would be based on the retail price of the car—$12,000, plus the full *retail* cost of the air—$800, plus tax and license—all of which amount to approximately $14,000. And 80% of that is $11,000. Therefore, the Smith s will have no trouble whatsoever borrowing the $7,100 they'll need.

Let me now throw in a word to the wise, however. When it comes to financing a car *never* assume. The plan you'll devise and all the other effort you will put into your car buy stand a good chance of going down the drain if you're suddenly stuck in the midst of the real dealing without the financing you *thought* you could get. When you enter a salesman's office you must be sure of *everything* or your bargaining position is weakened greatly. In order to get this confirmation, then, and at the same time verify how the increased down payment will reduce their monthly payments, Joan makes one last phone call to their credit union (or bank).

This time she tells the loan representative they have decided to buy a car that retails for approximately $11,000+ including tax and license. They'll only want to borrow about $7,100, however, and the rest they plan to make up in the down payment and trade-in equity. The reason for her call is to confirm *before* they go back to actually buy the car that the money is available. Also, she asks what the monthly payments for 36 months would be on that amount.

After the usual lender-borrower information is exchanged, Joan gets the confirmation and payments quoted somewhere in the area of $230 a month for 36 months. Since this fits the Smith's pocketbook much better, Joan confirms the fact they will take out the loan and let the representative know they will *first* close the deal to be sure of the exact amount, then come in to fill out the necessary paperwork and pick up the check.

As is now obvious, having completed these steps, Joan and Andy *know* beyond a shadow of a doubt what their own car is worth, what the car they plan to purchase is worth, how much money they will need to borrow, and the complete terms on which they will borrow the money. Put these facts all together and what they add up to is pride and self-confidence in their position as car buyers. They *know* they cannot be mislead or deceived as the unprepared buyer often is.

This self-confidence, however, does not mean the salesman will not try to deceive and talk more money out of them. The Smiths are well aware he will do exactly that. In order to help the Smiths learn how to deal first hand with his "persuasive techniques," let's take a moment to review a few more **BUYER'S COMMANDMENTS** which apply themselves specifically to sales office *action,* or what we've been referring to up to this point as the **REAL DEALING.**

1.  **BEGIN YOUR REAL DEALING WITH AN OFFER IMMEDIATELY AFTER THE TEST RIDE. START BY ASKING $500 MORE FOR YOUR OWN CAR THAN YOU KNOW IT'S WORTH, AND OFFERING $500 LESS THAN YOU PLAN TO PAY FOR THE DEALERSHIP'S CAR.**

One more test ride is essential for two reasons. First, it will give you a chance to drive the car again having cooled off for a day or two, and second, it will offer your "third baseman" (which we will discuss shortly) a chance to begin assisting you in your bargaining. When the ride is over, you should make your first firm offer as a starting point for the sales office *action.* The high/low technique mentioned is a traditional part of any bargaining process. The salesman will be attempting to work the exact same thing on you throughout the deal. His position will be to offer you the very *minimum* he feels he can get away with for your trade-in, and ask the *maximum* for his car. It is the unprepared and "easy" buyer who accepts the salesman's first offer as bottom line. The artistic buyer makes his or her own demands at the opposite ends of the scale and bargains to close the price gap to the amount preplanned.

2.  **DO NOT COMMIT YOURSELF TO DEALERSHIP FINANCING, BUT ACT OUT THE ENTIRE BAR GAINING PROCESS IMPLYING STRONGLY THAT THOSE ARE YOUR PLANS. THEN, IF THE DEALER SHIP CAN'T BEAT YOUR BEST LENDER'S OFFER, BECOME A CASH BUYER AT THE END OF THE DEAL.**

Remember, if the dealership feels you will finance through them, it means more money in their pocket, since they will attempt to charge you a higher interest rate than they originally paid on the money. And, remember these dollars, too, are considered profit by the sales force. Here's how this kind of thinking affects the bargaining process. If I as a salesman feel you will borrow money through me at an inflated interest rate, but at the same time you turn out to be a hard bargainer, I will be inclined to give in on some other aspect of the deal if I have to, and simply take the profit from you in an area you are unaware of. Thus, by playing out the bargaining process in this way you place another bargaining advantage in your favor. When you become a cash buyer in the end, though, that portion of the dealership's profit is placed right back in *your* wallet!

3. **OFFER YOUR DOWN PAYMENT IN THREE EQUAL PARTS AT THE APPROPRIATE PLACES IN THE BARGAINING PROCESS.**

By doing this, you will make the salesman (and in many cases a closer) feel they are slowly "grinding" more "across the board" profit from you as the deal goes on. To understand this, consider the fact that the dealership takes its own profit "off the top" of the deal. By increasing your down payment as you go, they see that cash in hand (immediate profit) multiplying before their eyes and are inclined to give in to your demands in return. If it's a used car you're buying, this technique carries still an added bit of leverage. You see, dealerships can only acquire financing on about 80% of the wholesale value of a used car and 90% (maximum) of the wholesale worth in new cars—plus tax and license. Your down payment, then becomes the difference between that and the actual wholesale price—e.g., the dealership's upfront profit !

4. **ESTABLISH A "REAL DEAL RANGE" FOR BOTH YOUR TRADE-IN AND THE NEW CAR.**

Most dealerships *will* sell their cars at a four or five hundred dollar profit (often less) provided they are handled properly. In the event you run into an exceptionally tough sales force, however, and are not able to get the deal down to your preplanned figures you should establish a range in which you will still close the deal. After all, why let an excellent deal go if it's not quite down to what you had planned?! As a rule, this real deal range should be between one and three hundred dollars, depending, again, on such things as how expensive the car you plan to purchase is, and how new and valuable your trade-in is. Remember, though, you will not bargain to get within this range. You will bargain for the figures you've planned on. The *only* time to consider closing the deal for other than these figures is if you feel you have pushed the dealership to the point of letting you walk away, and at that point they are just bordering the real deal range on a high demand car.

## 5.    BE PREPARED TO BARGAIN FOR PAYMENTS.

There are two important reasons for this. First, in most cases the salesman will be a payment bargainer since he is assuming you will be financing through the dealership. And if you *are* to play out the bargaining session on this assumption you must be genuinely *concerned* about those monthly payments, right? Second, there are times when a dealership *can* actually beat your other lender's terms. Should this turn out to be the case you must be prepared to change your plans and *really* let them carry the financing.

With these two thoughts in mind, remember the payments the salesman will quote you at first will probably be outrageously high. This is because he will start his figures at a high interest rate, and include extra profit. The interest you will take care of simply by demanding a lower **APR** based on your excellent credit rating. As for the profit, here's a handly little rule of thumb you can use. Three dollars multiplied by 36 months equals $108. So if it's 36 month contract you're dealing with there is $108 extra profit included for every $3.00 increase in your monthly payments. As an example, the Smiths *know* their monthly payments should in the end be $230. If at this point the salesman is saying they'll be $236 (a $6.00 increase) he will be including $216 *more* profit than you had figured. If he says $242, he's including an extra $418 and so on.

## 6.    VACILLATE IN THE BEGINNING, BUT INCREASE YOUR CONTROL AND DEMANDS AS THE BARGAINING PROCESS CONTINUES.

As I've mentioned, *control* is the name of the game in the car selling business. From the salesman's point of view, this means complete control throughout the bargaining process if he can pull it off. From your point of view, however, it is *advantageous* to begin with a passive, unemotional stance and become a tougher and more determined buyer as the deal progresses. The reason again is simple. If you walked back onto Jay Wilson's lot and played all your cards at once with one minimal profit demand, it's doubtful you'd get your deal, simply because Jay wouldn't have spent any of his time on you. Once he has worked on the deal, though, he has invested both his and his dealership's time and money. In addition, if you've played your cards patiently and in the proper order, he has *slowly* become aware that you are a real, live, on-the-spot buyer with a good deal of down payment money! Once in this position, both he and the dealership will become *tenacious* in attempting to bargain to the end in order to close the deal rather than let you walk off the lot and spend your dollars at another dealership.

## 7.  IF YOU ARE A LONE BUYER, BRING ALONG A "THIRD" BASEMAN."

And what exactly is a third baseman? A friend or relative who, unknown to the salesman, is again strengthening your position as a buyer by throwing "monkey wrenches" into the deal at the appropriate times to keep the salesman off balance. And what about the defintion of "monkey wrenches"? Well, consider the salesman's position when you return to the lot with a friend and he or she subtly begins to drop in negative comments such as, "Are you *sure* that brown color is the one you want?" or "I'll be perfectly honest with you, I think that sports car we looked at is much more your style—I mean, that's just my opinion . . . ." You can see the salesman will then be faced with two "buyers" to convince rather than one. Not only will this irritate him, it will extremely complicate his attempts to control you, thus keeping him working twice as hard and constantly off balance. The *key* to the third baseman's role is to be subtle, sincere, and not over do it enough for the salesman to either recognize what you're doing, or simply throw his hands up in the air in desperation and walk off mumbling four-letter words. In fact, to utilize your third basemen most effectively, you should preplan what the "monkey wrenches" will be and the cues on your part as to when to throw them into the deal. So be creative.

## 8. BRING ALONG A PENCIL, PAPER AND (IF POSSIBLE) A POCKET CALCULATOR.

Car salesmen work the kind of math you will be facing every day. They are both quick and accomplished at it—and in doing it in ways meant to confuse you. If you've brought a few math tools of your own you can do your own figuring to be sure he's right. At the same time pausing to refigure his numbers will tend to slow him down—again irritating and a detriment to his control.

## 9. PLAN TO SPEND APPROXIMATELY THREE HOURS BARGAINING.

This will give you ample time to reach the figures you've planned on. In addition, by *planning* on it, you will have nothing else pressing to do which might tend to make you want to hurry the deal or act impulsively. And consider this—if you pull off an excellent deal, your patience will have paid off to the tune of around $300 to $600 an hour!

## 10. BE PREPARED FOR THE LEGENDARY "CROSS-OVER."

Cross-over is a standard technique used by car salesmen, especially closers. It is simply a means of switching you from one portion of the deal (the trade-in value of you car, for instance) to another (your down payment) in order to confuse, fatigue and eventually break you down in one or more areas thereby increasing the profit. Your means of combating cross-over are: First, simply be aware it is going on; second, slow or stop the deal at cross-over points so you don't get confused and, third, stick to your guns on all phases of your plan, not allowing the sales force to bully you into giving in to their repeated pressure plays. Be patient with their game-playing and you will win a great victory as the deal comes to a close.

And with that our research is done. Joan and Andy Smith are now buyers in the know—artistic buyers who, from all the intelligence gathered, have developed the following plan:

1. To assure themselves they will be dealing with Jay Wilson himself, Joan will call Mr. Wilson in advance and arrange a day and time for she and Andy to return and "reconsider" the car in question.

2. When going in for the assault, Joan will assume the role of "third baseman." She and Andy will plan how and when she is to use the following "monkey wrenches."

   a. The back seat is small and uncomfortable;

   b. Only 18 miles per gallon is poor gas mileage in this age of repeated fuel shortages and rising prices;

   c. It is her "honest" opinion—and she will let it be known periodically—she and Andy should consider a compact car since they don't really need the room, the price tag would be less and the gas mileage is *twice* as good;

   d. In addition, it will be her job to keep a close eye and ear out for any figures that "accidentally" become inflated or "misplaced," and bring them to Andy's attention. And finally, should Andy begin to lose control or become stymied, pressured or bullied, Joan will distract the salesman by restating any of the established "monkey wrenches" until Andy has had time to gather his thoughts and decide on an appropriate defense.

As far as prices go, the Smiths will approach the deal this way:

1. Immediately following the test ride, they will make their first firm offer: They'll want $2,500 for their trade-in and are willing to pay $9,000 for the new car (this includes the air at half price but *not* the tax and license—that will come later on in the Deal). And if Jay can arrange those

73

figures our couple is perfectly willing to sign the papers *immediately*.

2. Once into the bargaining process Andy will offer $500 down. Later (when the salesman is insisting he *must* have more money), Andy will increase it to $1,000 demanding that Wilson reduce his price in return. He will save the last $500 until the deal is getting close to their preplanned figures, then offer it, and demand their bottom line selling price in return.

3. The Smiths will allow the following "real deal" ranges. Two hundred fifty dollars on the new car, which increases the bottom line purchase price from $9,250, and $250 on their trade-in which means the *least* they will accept is $1,750—and hence their reasoning. Since the maximum total increase is $500, this simply serves to put the air back at full retail price, but still leaves the car price an excellent deal.

4. And finally, they will bring paper, pencil and calculator along to slow or stop the deal at cross-overs or whenever they feel the need.

But so much for theory. Now, since Joan and Andy have gotten all their figures in order, developed the plan and are well aware of what they'll be up against, it's time for us in the audience to scoot forward in our seats and watch as they put it all together and go in for the assault!

# CHAPTER SIX

# 6
# THE ASSAULT

It is now a warm sunny Wednesday afternoon at 5:00 p.m. After an early dinner during which Joan and Andy reviewed Joan's "monkey wrench" procedure the couple have returned to the lot to meet Mr. Jay Wilson. To ensure themselves they'd be dealing with Wilson himself, Joan called in advance arranging the day and time to reconsider the two-door in question. Introductions are exchanged and Jay escorts Joan and Andy to the car, which "miraculously" has not been snatched up by one of those weekend buyers as he had predicted!

"Well," Andy asks Joan, "what do you think?"

"Yes," she replies. "I guess I like the color after all."

"This brown is real popular right now," Jay says.

"What kind of mileage does it get?" Joan asks casually.

"About 18 miles per gallon."

"How about with air conditioning?" Andy asks. "Will that hurt the mileage at all?"

"When you're using air you'll get a few miles less," he admits, "but air is a luxury and that's a price you'll pay for it in *any* car."

Joan prepares for her first pitch. "Sometimes I wonder if we should do without the luxury. The way gas prices are these days, 18 miles per gallon isn't that great. Some of the small cars get twice that!"

"That's true . . ." Andy responds, "vacillating" a bit strictly for Wilson's sake.

And he, of course, must now counter. "A compact isn't half the car you're getting here, though. This baby's made to last, to perform and give you full comfort at the same time. I'll tell you like it is, most of the compacts are cracker boxes. A few years on the road and they start falling to pieces."

Andy has listened to Jay's comments, of course, but still doesn't seem totally convinced; this makes it apparent that although they've returned and are definitely interested in buying the car, they're *still* not fully committed as a "today buyer."

To help the situation along a bit, Wilson suggests they resample some of that comfort and performance he was talking about by taking another test ride. The Smiths are in no rush, however. Andy pulls out the business card Wilson gave them on their last visit and glances at what he has written on it. "How about that offer you made us—half price on the air, does it still hold?"

At first he doesn't seem to recall. "Offer? What offer was that?"

"You offered us air at half price. See, I wrote it on your card."

"Well, I'm sure we can work *something* out," he says, avoiding the issue, "if you feel you'd like to buy the car today."

"Something?" Joan says, "or half price?"

"I'll put it this way, if you'd like to drive home in this car today we'll get air put in at half price!" At the same time, of course, he is figuring ways he can later work the $400 reduction back into the deal.

This test ride goes much like the first the Smith's took in this car. They are thoroughly sold on it, but they don't act like it at all. And Joan does her third baseman's job superbly by periodically throwing in more of her "monkey wrenches." When Andy asks her opinion, for instance, about the interior she responds with, "Nice . . . this back seat isn't the roomiest in the world, but it looks great!" Since they have no children she uses this also (as they had prearranged) to their advantage.

When the test ride is nearly over, she comments, "Andy, I'll be honest. It's a nice car, it really is, but I'm not sure. I mean it's just the two of us. I keep thinking maybe we should look around for something smaller. Think about it—we'd pay less money, get better gas mileage, and why be carting around all this extra space we really don't need. That is, unless you're planning on some additions to the family I don't know about."

Then the test ride is over, and Andy realizes it's time to set the stage for the upcoming sales office action. After walking around the car, thoroughly checking the trunk and engine, he makes his first play.

"I'll tell you what," he says suddenly in a very decisive manner, "we need $2,500 for the trade-in and if you can arrange to sell this one for $8,600 and let's see, the air at half price is $400, that comes to $9,000. Sell us this one for $9,000 and we'll sign the papers right now."

"You drive a hard bargain, Mr. Smith," he responds with a casual smile. He is adept at controlling the excitement he now feels, knowing he's got a couple of *real buyers* on his hands.

"Not a hard bargain, just a *fair* one."

"I'll tell you what, let's have a look at that trade-in. If it looks sharp, we'll write it up and see what the boss has to say."

Jay's office is a small, sterile cubicle with a seascape print on one wall, a desk, telephone, adding machine and a few chairs. He offers both the Smiths a cup of coffee. Andy accepts and Joan comments she'd really prefer a coke. Once this is arranged they settle down and as Wilson watches, Andy takes out his paper, pencil and calculator. "I'm terrible at figures," Andy says with a "typical" smile.

Wilson turns on his adding machine. "Okay, let's see. $2,500 for your trade-in . . . (He is now preparing to gently start slipping that first consumer carrot away.) I'll tell you right now, that's going to be a tough one, that make of yours really isn't selling right now. I don't know whether he'll buy it or not . . . ."

Joan picks up on this beautifully. "I saw one on a lot the other day advertised for $3,500."

Wilson shrugs. "Well, we'll give it a whirl." His adding machine and pencil now go rapidly to work. "Let's see, $9,000 for our car, then air at a discount, $400 . . ."

"No, that $9,000 was *including* air . . . ."

"Oh, okay, that's right. So we're talking $9,000 total." Then he looks Andy in the eye. "And how did you plan on paying for that, Mr. Smith? Cash? Check?"

"Well, no, we'll need to finance most of it."

"And are you going to arrange your own financing, or would you like us to take care of it?"

"I think I'd probably just as soon let you take care of the whole thing. We don't really care for all that hassle. If you can make my payments affordable, that is."

"No problem. Now there will be the credit application to fill out, and we'll need a down payment." He is again looking you straight in the eye trying to intimidate you, thus starting the "breaking down" of your defenses process.

After a moment's hesitation Joan asks, "How about our trade-in?"

"Sure, we may be able to take just that, but I'm going to be honest with you, I doubt I can get you the $2,500. And even if I do it's going to leave a pretty heavy balance. Let's see . . . your monthly payments will probably be around $480. Can you handle that?"

"$480!! Good Lord, no! $260 a month is more like it."

"Ma'am, there's no way I can get you down to $260 with that kind of a balance. We're talking $10,000 . . . . I may be able to work about, oh, say, $440 . . . maybe."

"We'd have to give up eating!"

"Well, ma'am, we've got to be realistic!"

At this point Andy moves in again to offer help. "Why is it so doubtful we'll get $2,500 for our car? I mean, if it's worth that . . ."

"Look," Wilson says, just a bit irritated now. "I'm not the type to pull your leg. I could sit here and say sure I'll get you the $2,500, but we'd just have to make it up some place in the deal. I mean, the car's got to be detailed, the fender's got to be fixed, we've got to wash it, polish it, run a complete mechanical inspection . . . All this adds up to money, and let's face it, at that price we'll have a tough time making a dime on it. I mean, we've got to be realistic. It's simple. To bring your payments down, we'll need some *money* down."

"Okay," Andy concedes, "I'll give you $500 down *plus* my $2,500 trade-in, and as far as I'm concerned that should put a pretty good dent in it."

"Okay, let's see . . . down payment . . . $500. That brings the balance to $8,500. If you'll just fill out this credit application, I'll run this by the boss and we'll see where we stand . . . ."

The credit application asks the standard questions: Where they work? How much they make? What are their expenses? Assets? Deficits? What other loans are they now paying on? Have they ever had anything repossessed? Claimed bankruptcy? Their bank account numbers, etc., etc.,—in short, a detailed history of the Smith's adult financial life.

And just when they are in the midst of struggling through it (he has probably timed it this way to get our couple in a position of being less able to concentrate on the issue at hand) Wilson re-enters. His look is one of despair. He is now a "loyal friend" caught between a rock (the boss) and a hard place (Joan and Andy)—or so he would have them *think*.

Rather than play into his hands and try to do the remainder of the credit application at the same time they're bargaining, our couple simply put it aside.

"Well," Joan asks, "how'd we do?"

"You remember what I said about being realistic . . .? Well, I'll put it this way. The boss is a very realistic man—if you know what I mean."

Joan turns to Andy, "That sounds like bad news to me."

"Here's where we're at: I can get you $600 for your trade-in and we've got to have $11,000 for our car—that's with the air at half price. As far as payments go, you're in luck. I can get you in the area of $230 with no problem—on a 48-month contract."

Both Joan and Andy realize it's still too early to become overly demanding, but they've got to get that $600 figure up. The 48-month contract they'll deal with in a minute. "Why only $600 for our car?" Andy asks politely.

"Because, Mr. Smith, that's what it's worth."

81

"But they're selling for a lot more. I've checked around."

"The people selling them may be *asking* a lot more. What they're *selling* for is a different story. I'm being honest with you, $600 is a perfectly realistic price for it."

"Realistic?" Andy responds calmly, but obviously disturbed. "You keep saying realistic, but what you mean is ridiculous!! My car is worth twice that figure—more . . . ."

"Look, Mr. Smith, the simple fact is we're here to make a profit, and it's got to come from somewhere. Now what I *can* do is probably get our five year special warranty thrown in at maybe half price—another $200 bucks—with that, but that's really the best I can do."

"No," Andy says, becoming firm. "I don't care for any warranties. And I want a 36-month contract, by the way— not 48."

"Well, maybe I can work taking the $200 out of the deal anyway, but . . . A gift to you!"

"You're taking advantage. Profit? Okay, let's talk about profit. If you get our car at $600, you're going to wash and vacuum it, adjust it to the wholesale price of $2,000, tack on another $1000, and sell it for $3,000. There's two thousand dollars + profit right there, and that's not including the profit you'll get on the new car!! No, that's crazy . . . We've got to have $2,000 for it at least. And that's still giving you *plenty* of profit."

"Mr. Smith, there's no way we could sell your car for $3,000. They're just not selling for that! And the first thing we'd have to do is spend $500 getting the front fender fixed and painted."

"That's a hundred at the most. I priced it."

From the trend of this conversation, Jay begins to see he's going to have a tough time snowing these two. It's becoming apparent they know a good deal about car prices. So he decides to give a little in a grand gesture of good will.

"I'll tell you what. I'll get you $750 for it, but that's the best I can do. Man, I've got to make some kind of commission on this deal! And, okay, I can probably get a discount past the boss and bring your payments down to . . . about $290 on 36 months."

"Listen," Andy says, "Okay, we'll take $1750 for our trade-in, but you'll have to take more off that new car. You're taking advantage of me on that too; $290 a month is outrageous."

"Mr. Smith, I keep trying to make you understand—nobody's taking advantage of you! It's my business to know car prices. Believe me, I'm being totally honest when I say your car is not *worth* $1750."

"Well, it's worth more than $1,500," Joan interjects.

"Sure it is," Andy says.

"Look, if I'm lucky—and I mean lucky—I can get you $800 for it, but I really doubt it. Let me explain again, Mr. Smith. I'm not pulling your leg, honest to God. We've *got* to make some money some place in the deal. I mean I got kids. And, Hell, you're telling me you want my car at below wholesale?! Remember we owe the bank for that car. No way are we going to sell it at a loss."

Since Andy now has him within $900 of what they had planned for their trade-in, he decides to leave it at that for the moment and make Wilson do a little work. He first writes the $800 figure on his piece of paper with the large words *TRADE-IN* next to it and writes below $2,000 wholesale worth. This is to make it apparent to all they've reached that figure but the real wholesale figure is known. Then he sits back in his chair and asks, "I can't quite understand this. Please explain it. How *exactly* are you losing money when, the way I see it, you're making . . . let's see, at $800 for our trade-in . . . a quick $3,000 profit at *least* as soon as you mark it up and sell it. And how do you figure you're selling *your* car at a loss?"

"Mr. Smith, that car wholesales for $11,000 the way it sits there! Put air in and there's another $900. Now, by my math this comes out to $11,900—which means with the deal I offered you we'll *still* come away with only pennies on it! And if we pick yours up at $1,500, by the time we get it ready for the line we're talking $2,500 in it—minimum. Then, it may sit out there for months, maybe years—Hell, it may never sell! Now, let's face it, we can't make any money that way!"

"Like I said, honey," Joan says, "what we need is a compact."

"Maybe so . . ." Andy says and sits back "thinking" it over seriously.

But Jay's job is twofold. He's got to talk you into a profitable offer, *without* letting the deal go to another lot. So he drops in a casual, "Now, don't get me wrong, we want to sell you the car, but man, you've got to be reasonable. I'll tell you what. If I can get your payments down to . . . let's say $392 how's that?"

The Smiths have been in Jay's office for over an hour now. Andy decides to get a little huffy and start becoming more demanding. "Let's back up a bit. You're saying the car wholesales for $11,000. That's not true. We both know it wholesales for $8,600. I checked on that, too. And then the air. Now *you* offered that to me at half price. And it retails for $800. not $900. You also said you wanted to sell me the car. Well, I want to buy it. But I *don't* want to play games. I really don't have time for that. Now you also say let's be realistic—you need more money. Okay. I'll give you $9,500 for it—and you give me $1,750 for my trade-in. There's a minimum of $500 profit in that. If you *really* want to sell the car, write it up with payments around $230 a month, get your boss to okay it, and I'll sign the papers and write you a down payment check right now."

After this little display of buyer confidence and knowledge, Jay *knows* he's dealing with a shrewd buyer and one in the know. He also knows, that Andy and Joan are **REAL BUYERS**. And that alone will keep him fighting to the end before letting them and the deal walk out the door. He decides he needs a break to reorganize his thoughts and formulate more strategy. "Okay," he says, "we'll try it." He writes up the deal as Andy has just stated and gets up. "I'll give it my best shot . . ."

Once he gets into the sales manager's office, though, his best shot goes something like this:

"Here's what they want, Jim. They're tough. But they're buyers!"

"Do they have cash down?"

"Yeah—$500."

84

"$500! Hell, we've got to get more than that out of 'em. Tell them we need more bucks before we can start talking the kind of payments they want. Then lay dealer prep. on them and installation problems with the air. We've got to have it air freighted in from "Kalamazoo" or something. Will they buy that?"

"I don't know. They're both pretty savvy."

"Can you handle 'em?"

"I think so."

"Do you want me to send Bill in to give you a hand?"

"No. Let me have another shot at 'em. I'll get 'em up."

"Okay, listen, have a cup of coffee and relax for a minute— let them stew a little. Then go back in and do it to 'em. And if you need Bill, let me know—but don't lose 'em!!"

"Sure."

While having that cup of coffee, Jay looks up at the monthly sales chart on the office wall. His name is second from the bottom. Not for long, though, he decides. He will close this deal no matter what—and that will just be the beginning . . . .

This time when he returns the credit application is completed and Joan and Andy are having a casual conversation about a friend's sports car.

"Sorry, folks," he says, "but he won't do it."

"Why not?" Joan asks.

"Well, for two reasons mainly. And I'm afraid I've got to apologize for one, since it was my mistake."

At this, Joan stirs in her chair and gives Jay a look that says, *Okay, what kind of a line is coming now?*

"You see, I forgot to account for the fact that the air conditioning has to be delivered from the factory. We don't keep the units here in our service department. Now there's two ways we can do it. If you need it fast we'll get it in air freight*4 1—that's $500. Or if you can wait a week for it we can have it trucked in for $75."

"And the other problem?"

"The other problem, *Mr. Smith*, is simply that we need more money. You've got to understand we have to pay the bank on these cars. That's cash out of our pockets. And if we can't get some profit out of the deal we just can't let the car go. Now the best I can do is $900 for your car and $11,000 for us, plus delivery of that air. Monthly, I can knock it down to . . . $272."

******goes with above copy

*4   A fictitious illustration to display the creativeness of the salesman and
     his desperate need to sell, **TODAY!**

Now Andy's got to do some quick thinking. Delivery of the air is something he's really not sure about. He figures it's probably another bogus charge to get more profit into the deal, but he can't be sure. Wilson is looking him straight in the eye, pressuring him for a quick, *impulsive* decision. He senses he's just gotten control. Rather than *make* that impulsive decision, Andy simply tells him he'd like to do some figuring. After doing so for five minutes (during which time Joan has kept him busy with an assortment of questions) he decides not to go for it— at least not without a fight.

"No," he says, "a week is too long to wait for the air. I'd like it right away, but that $500 delivery isn't fair and I told you we can't afford those kinds of payments. Listen. Okay, I'll give you (he now pauses again to figure on his calculator) $9,400 for your car. But I want $1,750 for mine and I need my payments lower."

"Sir, I can't lower your payments without more money! I just can't do it!"

After "thinking" this over, Andy finally says, "Okay, I'll do one *more* thing. I'll give you . . . let's see, I said $500 . . . I'll give you $1,000 down right now, today. Now at $1,000 down and $1,750 for my car, that's $2,750 off the balance, a thousand of which you'll get as money in your pocket—*right now!*"

Now Jay goes to his adding machine and whips out some new figures. He's delighted at having just gotten the additional $500 down, but he's going to press for more. He figures he'll do it with a little "cross over" from trade-in to delivery charges on the air. "Okay," he says, "listen. I'll see if I can get you the $1,500 for your car, but I can't pay delivery on the air— I mean, I'm already giving it to you at half what it's worth!"

Before Andy does anything else he realizes he must now lock in that $1,500 for the trade-in as established bottom line. On the paper in front of him he *scratches out* the large letters and numbers "TRADE-IN $800"—and at the same time writes in these NEW figures, "Okay trade-in, $1,500. Now, what does that come out to monthly with a thousand down?"

Jay goes back to the machine again and working with an 18% APR comes up with a monthly figure of only $285.

When Joan hears this she becomes openly angry. "$285. You're kidding. It was $272 a minute ago before we gave you $500 more down!"

"Okay, let's see. I'll tell you what. I'll work another discount in for you, if I can get it by the boss. How about . . . $262?"

"That's better, but I still don't think we can afford it." And now she sees an opening to start working themselves in as cash buyers. "We can get lower payments from the bank, honey. Maybe we should finance it through them."

Again, Andy "thinks" it over. "Maybe so... Something's wrong, though. It doesn't seem like we should be paying that much monthly. What kind of figures did you use?"

"What do you mean, what kind of figures?" Jay says defensively. "I do this every day, sir. I *know* what the figures are."

"I'm sure you do," Andy says politely, "but it just seems high." He knows full well Wilson is probably working with an inflated interest rate and perhaps a few other inflated figures, too. To press the issue, though, would be backing Wilson into a corner—a mistake. Instead he decides to apply pressure in another way.

A glance at his watch tells him nearly two hours have passed since the couple entered his office. Time to get tough.

Andy suddenly gets extremely serious and contemplative. He is going to either bring the deal down or walk out. He stands up and motions to Joan. "Look," he says to Wilson. "We're sorry for having taken up so much of your time, but I really don't feel we're getting fair treatment on this. I've seen on TV how some lots operate and I think it's best we just think it over and check some other dealerships . . . ."

Jay now envisions all the extra profit he has worked into the deal suddenly going down the drain! He also sees his name again in chalk on the bottom of that chart. He's not about to let these two get away. But he's *got* to hold his composure. He can't let them see how badly he wants to sell the deal.

"Listen, Mr. and Mrs. Smith," he says. "My boss insists on a high degree of integrity here and if you two feel you've been wronged, my apologies. But, honestly, you haven't. Now, if you feel you'd like to shop some more, fine, but I'll tell you what. Since it was my mistake on the air, I'll deduct the delivery on it. I'll just take the difference out of my commissions. And since you *are* an excellent credit risk I'll see if we can get those monthly payments down a bit more. How about it? Let me write it up and try it on him. What have you got to lose?"

Hesitantly, the couple agree and Wilson furiously goes to work rewriting the deal—now within reach of what they've preplanned. If Wilson or a closer should come back with a "no" this time, Andy figures he'll throw in the final $500 down, give in for another $100 or $150 on the price, then say that's it.

To help reinforce the point, however, when Wilson leaves with the new deal, he and Joan also *leave*. They walk out of the showroom and mill about looking over the new car, giving the impression that although they've given in, they may *still* be contemplating walking off the lot.

Meanwhile, back in the sales office, something like this is going on. Since Wilson realized he had lost quite a bit of *control* in that last awkward bit of conversation, and since Joan and Andy scared the *devil* out of him by threatening to leave, he has decided to let Bill—a closer—take over. He tells Bill all that has transpired—that the couple almost walked out. He mentions also they will *definitely* buy today if he can lock in the deal. Bill checks all the figures and decides to ask for more down, drop the interest rate to 15%, and try to get away with less for the trade-in.

When he's got his strategy all figured, he comes to Wilson's office to introduce himself, but finds it vacant. His first thought is the Smiths decided to just forget it after all. Then, he sees they're at the car. He realizes it's not too late and comes rushing out.

His first play is to apologize for the mistake Wilson has made and assure the couple that all the salesmen who work for him are required to *not* make such mistakes. This, then, is the reason he's decided to agree to Jay's offer to have the delivery charge taken out of his monthly commissions (a sales ploy). The fact is he's new and he has to learn—one way or another. If they'd care to step back into the office he's sure he can write the deal up agreeable to all!

Once back in the office, though, he's not quite so cordial. He becomes very business-like. His intent, the Smiths are fully aware, is to get more money into the deal, somehow, without losing them. After a bit of paper work, calculating and talking of lowering the payments, he comes to the $1,500 for their trade-in.

"Mr. Smith," he says, "now I'll be glad to deduct the mistake Jay made in his figuring on the air, but I'm afraid he's mis appraised your trade in, too. There's just no way I can get you $1,500 for your car. I mean, *you've* got to be realistic with us, too."

"I think that's perfectly realistic!" Joan says. "And it's what he offered us."

"Did he tell you what we do with most of our trade-ins?" Bill asks.

"No, he didn't, but we know what you do with them. You add on another $1,000 or $1,500 and sell them."

Bill chuckles. "Well, I wish it were that easy! And I'll be honest with you, with some cars it is. But with cars like yours, rather than put the time and money into them, we just wholesale them out to used car lots. We don't have the time or space to hold them. If we get one that's sharp—just about ready to go on the lot, we'll keep it, but yours, well, the dent, and that mileage . . . No, we'll just wholesale it out. And I'll be really honest with you, I doubt we can get $1000 for it wholesale. I *will* take that risk, though. I can give you a flat $1000."

"Look," Andy counters, "we really don't care how you handle that car once it's yours, but it lists for $2,000 *Bluebook* wholesale and we're willing to deduct $250 for the dent in the fender. We need $1,750 for it."

"Well, it's simple then. If I give you the $1,750, I've got to get $700 somewhere else in the deal. I mean, I'm being truthful with you, folks. We're *not making any money* here and that's what we're in business for. Let's face it, we're selling the car low as it is! And we've taken $100 more out of the deal for Mr. Wilson's miscalculation! Now you're demanding an extra $750 for your car."

"We're not demanding an *extra* $750! We're demanding what my car is worth and what Wilson agreed to pay for it!"

"Folks, I just can't do it. We've got to have more money. Can you give me more down?"

"I already increased it to $ 1,000. What more do you want?"

"Like I said, I just want to make an honest profit. And I can't let the car go unless I do. At $1,000 down I can get you into it for . . . let's see . . . I can give you one final discount (the 15% APR instead of 18%). I'll let you have it for $291 a month. I'm afraid that's the bottom line."

"How much more down would it take to get our payments down to $230?"

". . . $750 to $1,000."

"No way we can do that," Joan says.

"Then, ma'am, I can't sell you the car. Not unless you want to go 48 months. Then I can get you into that range."

Now the stage is set for the Smiths last ace in the hole. Bill wants more money and they are going to give it to him (as they had planned in advance, of course) but in exchange they are going to demand something also—the deal they planned for.

"How much is tax and license?" Andy asks.

Bill checks a few charts and the adding machine goes to work. "About $1,000."

"Okay, listen," Andy says with utter finality. "You people keep saying you need more money. I told you I'd give you $1,000 down and as far as I'm concerned that gives you plenty of money, but I'll increase it *again*. I'll give you $1,500 down, another $500. But, I want $1,750 for my car and I'll buy yours—

tax, license, and air included—the *entire* deal for $10,500. And you'll have to get the payments down to $254."

Bill does more figuring. "Make it $11,000 and ... okay, I can work $250 a month. And you folks can drive out of here in your brand new car."

"$10,500." Andy reaches into his pocket. "I'll write you a check for the $1,500 Down payment right now!"

"I can go $10,600. That's it. I'll have to let you go."

Since they are now very close to their planned deal (well within their **REAL DEAL RANGE**) and they realize they've pushed it about as far as they can, they concede.

"You've got a deal," Andy says. Then he immediately finalizes the figures verbally and on his paper—"Trade in, $1,750; Down Payment, $1,500; New Car Price—Tax, License, Air Included—$10,600; and Monthly Payments, $254.

## Bank Terms for $7,350
## months of contract

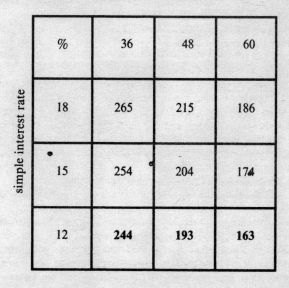

| % | 36 | 48 | 60 |
|---|----|----|----|
| 18 | 265 | 215 | 186 |
| 15 | 254 | 204 | 174 |
| 12 | **244** | **193** | **163** |

simple interest rate

# CHAPTER SEVEN

# 7

# THE CONTRACT

Well, they've done it! Step four of the buyer's art—Bargain! Bargain! Bargain!—is now complete. Before our couple let down their guard, however, and begin to pat each other on the back, they have one more extremely critical bit of business to take care of—the signing of the contract. Why so critical? For the simple reason that the excellent deal they have just closed could well go down the tubes if a close eye is not kept on what is contained in the contract they must still sign. Believe it or not, many a buyer has settled verbally on an agreed set of closing figures and left the sales office owing hundreds of dollars more than they thought. It is for this reason the artistic buyer *never* considers an excellent deal finalized until after signing the contract.

With this in mind, before returning for the closing act of "Car Wars," we are going to pass on four more **Buyer's Commandments** in advance. Remember, they are of prime importance, so be prepared to follow them to the letter!

1.  **I WILL BE SURE ALL OF THE FIGURES THE DEALERSHIP AND I HAVE AGREED UPON ARE SHOWN IN WRITING AND IN THEIR CORRECT PLACES.**

Sound simple? Consider that car salesmen, and *especially* closers, are masters at the art of lickety-split paper work, confusing math and double-talk. Also, consider this: if you have talked a dealership into an extremely good deal, the contract is their *last* chance to somehow "squeeze" in a bit more profit. While reputable dealerships will not resort to contact "trickery," many "questionable" ones have been known to do so.

There are several ways of distracting a buyer during a contract reading you should know about. The first is the old "change the subject fast if the buyer sees something he or she shouldn't" technique. And your means of combating it? simple. Stop everything immediately if there is anything you don't understand on the contract and don't continue until it is fully and understandably explained. This brings us to the second Sales team technique—the "stupid buyer's ego" play. Here's how it's done. You ask a question about some figure on the contract. The closer responds with a fast bit of double-talk and at the same time implies you're stupid if you don't understand what he is saying. Then he hurries on to something else. Your means of combating this one starts by keeping this thought in mind. You are not a contract expert, a math whiz nor a master of the art of persuasion. Therefore, you are not stupid even if you don't understand something the closer says. It's the buyers who let what he says go *unquestioned* who fall into this category and are later subject to Buyer's Remorse. So, again, don't let the deal proceed until you *do* understand completely—even if it takes ten explanations!

## 2. I WILL BE SURE ANY AND ALL PROMISES THE DEALERSHIP HAS MADE ARE SPECIFICALLY STATED ON THE CONTRACT IN WRITING.

The salesman or closer may come up with any number of excuses why *not* to do this, all of which boil down to the same thing—an *out*. If the contract states "factory air to be installed by June 5, 19—" your factory air will be installed by that date. If it says nothing at all or something like "air included" (which could be construed to mean any number of things) when you return to have the air installed there's a good chance the double-talk and excuses will start. And they may *never* end until you finally give up and say the heck with the whole thing!

## 3. I WILL BE ON THE LOOKOUT FOR ADDED DOLLARS.

This commandment ties in closely with number one, but it's important to emphasize that besides the figures being correct and where they should be, they must also be the *only* figures on the contract. If something shows up that shouldn't be there, the salesman may use the same techniques previously mentioned to try to cover it up and hurry you on to another subject. Your means of dealing with this kind of treatment are also the same. Stop everything, ask for and *get* an explanation you fully understand before letting the deal continue. Then demand that the extra dollars, as official and inescapable as they may be made to sound, be taken out of the deal and off your contract. If you have just agreed on a complete *bottom line* deal that's what you should get.

## 4. I WILL BE SURE TO SIGN THE CONTRACT BEFORE LEAVING THE LOT.

As was mentioned earlier, the deal you've bargained for is not official or *binding* until it is all in writing on the contract and signed by you and the salesmanager. More than a few buyers have driven off the lot with a car, taken it home, test driven it for 10 days, shown the neighbors, and in essence let it become *their own brand new car* without a signed contract. Then when they do return to the lot to do the signing, for one "unfortunate" reason or another things have changed. An additional $50, $100 or even $500 has now become necessary in order to purchase the car. In the meantime, their trade-in has been sold! And without a signed contract, it's perfectly legal.

And with that, the stage is set for our closing act. Here's the scene: The paperwork (a Worksheet which *looks* like a contract) is on the desk, and Bill is prepared to "write it up." Sitting across from him are Joan and Andy. They both have two final goals to accomplish: first and foremost, to get a contract signed which finalizes their deal as soon as possible; second, they must now, in a convincing and graceful way, become cash buyers before they sign.

"So, what," Joan asks, "are the payments going to be?"

"$254 a month," Andy responds, "guess it's time to tighten up the budget."

Bill has been busily writing on the worksheet. At this, however, he stops. "You know, if that's too tough to live with we can still work a 48 month contract. That'll knock the payments down to around . . . $215. I mean, it's up to you, but I'd make it as easy on myself as I could." His reasoning, of course, for giving our couple this "helpful" bit of advice is, again, profit. If the contract changes to 48 months, the **APR** goes up (as high as he can manage to get it) and the dealership gets a last bit of "frosting on the cake."

Andy has no intention whatsoever in doing it, but he turns to Joan, "What do you think? $215 would be a lot easier to live with."(See payment chart at end of last chapter. Is salesman trying to take more profit? How much?)

"I already told you what I think, honey. I think we should borrow the money from the credit union. I mean, money is money!"

"I know, but that's such a hassle!"

Bill, meanwhile, has returned to the contract. Andy now responds to his question. "No, 48 months is too long. I think we'll just stay with the $254. We'll just have to tighten up a bit"

"Fine," Bill says, writing away.

Just then Joan suddenly spies something on the Worksheet that doesn't look quite right. There is a $128 figure on one of the dotted lines. Since this doesn't ring a bell, she decides to stop the action and find out what it's all about

"Excuse me," she says, pointing a pencil at the figure. "What's the $128? It's not our payments, is it?"

Bill's verbiage now speeds up a bit. "That's the discount for the air installation. You're really making out here, I'll tell you." At the same time he says this, he tends to cover the Worksheet a bit with his hand, and he follows with an immediate,

"Let's see, we said $2,000 down. Will that be cash or check, Mr. Smith?"

"Just a minute," Joan says firmly. Let's clarify something. Back up a bit. First, the down was $1,500, not $2,000. But let's forget that for a minute, and talk about this discount. What *exactly* does that mean?"

"Oh, sure, yeah, it's a special discount we offer our customers who have items put in that aren't factory installed . . . . You know, that $1,500 may change the figures here a bit. I'm not really sure we can get you off at $254 a month" This last comment about the payments is, of course, meant to take Joan and Andy's attention *away* from the $128 "discount." If they buy it, after two or three minutes of conversation, they will have forgotten about the $128 figure. The monthly payments will be $254, spouts the salesman." But they don't buy it!

"Listen," Andy says, "we don't want to talk about anything else until we're totally clear on this $128. Now, please explain."

Joan follows up immediately with, "Sounds to me like a discount on some sort of charge to install the air conditioning."

"Right," Bill says.

"But you never *said* anything about an installation charge to begin with! That's not part of the deal."

"Well, that's a standard fact of life, Mrs. Smith. I mean, it takes trained men to put the equipment in. And besides, you're getting off cheap and I mean it. It's usually over $150. At $128 you're getting it at cost."

"Oh, I see. Then the $128 isn't a *discount* at all, it's an *extra* charge. No. We agreed on a *complete, bottom line price* and that's what we want on the contract before we'll sign it. And this is the second time you've tried to do this. Is this the "fair" treatment you talked about?"

"Mrs. Smith, I'm not trying to be rude, but ma'am, you're expecting blood from us! I mean, we can't just go around dropping charges like that!"

"As far as I'm concerned," Andy says firmly, "you can't just go around dropping charges *into* the contract like that either. Now, you've been in this business a long time and you know *exactly* what charges are involved with the air conditioning. You also know you should have brought them up when we were *discussing* the deal, not after we agreed on a bottom line, *full and complete price*. So if you want to sell us the car, honor the agreement and write it up that way!"

Now, shaking his head as if Joan and Andy are so "tight" they've just taken the food from his children's mouths, Bill realizes he has no choice but to drop the charges, and he does so. He also realizes these two are a bit too sharp to let him slip anything in, so he'd better stop trying to take our couple "for a ride" and simply write up the deal as they've agreed. The Worksheet goes in the wastepaper basket and he pulls a new one from his desk.

And now Joan and Andy both sense it's time to pull off their final bit of preplanned strategy. "And one other thing," Andy says, "if the payments do go up like you mentioned a bit earlier, we'll just have to borrow the money some other place, probably from the credit union. We can't afford any more than $254."

At this Bill does a bit of math and finally comes to the conclusion he has made a "mistake," the payments will indeed be $254.

Then Joan takes over, "Honey, I'll be honest with you. I don't understand why we have to pay that much to begin with. I mean, our credit rating is excellent." Then to Bill, "What kind of interest are we paying?"

"Fifteen percent," Bill says.

"Is that the **APR?**"

"Ah . . . no . . . The **APR** is a little higher."

"Why can't you drop it to 12%? We're obviously not a risk?"

"Because we've already dropped it as low as we can go, ma'am. We've got to at least break *even* on the money."

At this Joan turns to Andy. "You know Ann Lawrence, don't you?"

"Yes."

"Well, she just got a car loan last month from the credit union and I'm sure it was 12%. What the heck, we've got to go down and sign a few papers, but that's 3% difference, and 3% is money in our pockets!"

100

". . . That's true," Andy says, obviously "contemplating" changing his mind.

"I'll tell you," Bill interjects. "There's no way she could have gotten that money at 12%. *Nobody's* lending that cheap. And think about this. If you *do* borrow from a credit union, your borrowing power with them is locked up for three years."

"What do you mean?" Andy asks

"I mean if an emergency comes up and you two need to borrow some cash quick, they won't give you a dime! You'll be hung out to dry!"

Andy thinks that one over for a moment. "Let me ask you this, though. If I *did* get the money someplace else, how long would we have to get you the balance?"

"We'd need it within a week. And that brings up another problem. Getting money out of credit unions is usually a long. drawn out process."

"Why?"

"Because they've got so many rules and government restrictions. I'll tell you, it involves more red tape than you can believe."

"And what if it took, let's say, ten days or two weeks to get it, could you . . ."

"Then your contract becomes due and payable in full, you stand a chance of losing your car, plus your credit rating! Either that or finance through us."

"Losing the car! You mean you'd make us pay the contract in full over a couple of days delay?"

"Mrs. Smith, I don't think you quite understand. This is a binding contract and there's a lot of money involved here. Now . . ."

"And 15% is the best you can do?"

"Look, I'll tell you what. Your credit is excellent. If you two can give me another $500 down, I'll get you a special discount on it from the "factory". We'll let the money go for 9% and, I mean it, that's the best I can do! And probably as good as any credit union could. The auto factory wants to sell their cars too!"

This has caught Joan by surprise. She had never imagined a dealership could get below the credit union figures! But since this is one of these rare occasions, it deserves some thought—some *serious* thought.

Is 3%, for instance, worth going back to the credit union for? And can the Smiths afford another $500 down? And is there a chance Bill will still loan the money at 9% if they tell him they can't afford the extra $500? After a moment's thought, she decides to try for the 9% *without* more money down. And in doing so, she displays another admirable trait of the artistic buyer—flexibility—being prepared to take advantage of an option in the plan, provided it *enhances* the deal.

"No . . . we can't afford $500 more," she states. "But since our credit is excellent you can still give us the discount."

"Sorry. But I can't—not unless I show more cash in the deal."

"What would it do to our monthly payments?"

"Let's see . . . ," he says, going to work on his calculator, ". . . how does $231 sound for 36 months?"

"We can give you another $100 cash, $1,600 down total, and that's it."

"Make it $ 1,850," Bill says.

Andy now picks up on what's happening and gets into the action. "$1,600 and you've got a deal," he says with utter finality.

"No. I've got to have at *least* $ 1,800."

"Okay, just write the whole deal up for cash. We'll borrow from the credit union and get you the balance in a week."

"Mr. and Mrs. Smith," Bill says (and for once he *is* totally sincere), "you two drive one *hell* of a bargain, and I mean it! You got a deal. $1,600 down and I'll get you the money at 9%."

"Don't worry," Joan says with a casual, "typical" buyer's smile, "you'll make it up on the other 95% of people who don't know anything about buying a car."

The fact that Bill knows you are perfectly right is his only consolation at this moment. All he wants to do now is write it up and get one of the shrewdest couples he's run into in years out of his hair, off his back, and out of his office!

A *real* contract is now produced and written up. It reads properly—from top to bottom. After looking it over carefully Andy picks up the pen to sign it. Suddenly he realizes there *is* one more thing he's forgotten.

"Oh, the air conditioning. How soon can it be installed?"

Bill calls the service department and asks for a date. Then he cups his hand over the transmitter and says, "How about next Monday, that's five days?"

"Fine"

Bill confirms the appointment and hangs up.

"We'd like that in writing on the contract, too," Joan says.

"The appointment is made, Mrs. Smith. I mean, there's no problem, believe me!"

"I'm sure there's not," Andy answers, "but Joan and I always get everything in writing. We've known people who didn't and were sorry about it later"

"Okay," Bill says and takes the contract.

This time when it's returned, "Air conditioning to be installed on July 5th" has been included. Our couple now confidently apply their signatures and our audience goes wild. The applause is still going strong when the curtain closes for the final time . . . .

# CHAPTER EIGHT

# IN A NUTSHELL

The following outline will serve as a checklist for your own
artistic auto purchase. It briefly recaps all of the steps followed
by Andy and Joan in "Car Wars." Chapter and page number,
are included with each category in case you'd care to reread
that portion of **THE BUYER'S ART** and refresh your memory
in greater depth. Remember—follow these steps to the letter
and the three or four hours you spend bargaining for your
next car will pay off to the tune of literally hundreds of dollars
an hour! In addition, for what may be the first time in your
life you will actually *enjoy* dealing with that infamous "legend
of the lots" himself . . . *the car salesman!*

## THE ARTISTIC BUYER'S CHECKLIST

I.  Make a tentative choice as to the type of car you're in
    the market for; *e.g.* sports car, station wagon, pickup, etc.,
    and any extras you want to include. When doing so,
    consider the following guidelines:

    A.  Yours and your family's needs;

    B.  Your lifestyle;

    C.  Finances.                    *(Chapter 3, pages 36-41)*

II. Gather your "soft intelligence" as follows:

A. Gain a feel for the marketplace by reading the car ads section of your local newspaper;

B. Gain a feel for the quality of the cars you may be considering by reading current periodicals, such as **CONSUMER REPORTS, CHANGING TIMES, MOTOR TREND**, etc.

C. Call several lenders and secure the following information:

1. Their **APR** on car loans;
2. How much they will lend (% of car loan);
3. How much your approximate loan amount works out to in terms of monthly payments;
4. The total dollar payback;
5. The wholesale value of your trade-in;
6. The wholesale and retail value of one of the cars you are considering.

*(Chapter 3, pages 35-41)*

D. With the information you have just secured, figure the following:

1. Your cheapest lender;
2. The approximate down payment you will need;
3. The approximate monthly payments you can live with.

*(Chapter 3, pages 40-41)*

III. Gather your "hard intelligence" as follows:

A. Narrow your choice of cars to one or two;

B. Visit a minimum of three lots and test drive those cars you are considering;

C. Attempt to locate a new salesman;

D. Make mental note of selling techniques (high pressure, type, smooth talker, etc.)

E. "Vacillate" to imply you *might* just buy today;

F. Ask for the salesman's card and write any "offers" he makes you on the back;

G. Do not enter the sales office.

*(Chapter 4, pages 48-49)*

IV. Develop your plan as follows:

A. Decide on the car you will buy;

B. Call your cheapest lender and confirm the following:

1. The exact wholesale value of the car you will buy;
2. The exact amount of your loan;
3. Your exact monthly payments;
4. The fact that you will definitely take out the loan and you will call back to do so before buying the car.

*(Chapter 5, pages 66-69)*

C. With the figures you now have, calculate the following:

1. The dollar amount and % profit you will allow the dealership;
2. The total tax and license;
3. The bottom line price you will pay for the car;
4. The total amount you will ask for your trade-in;
5. The exact down payment you will offer;
6. Establish real deal ranges for both your trade-in and the car you will purchase.

*(Chapter 5, pages 63-66)*

D. Enlist the help of a "third baseman" and establish a list of "monkey wrenches" he or she will use to assist in keeping the salesman off balance.

*(Chapter 5, pages 71-72)*

E. Decide on a day and time for your purchase and call to confirm an appointment with your salesman.

V. When you go in for the "assault" remember:

A. Take a final test ride;

B. After the test ride make your initial offer as follows:

1. Offer approximately $500 below your preplanned bottom line figure for the car you will buy;
2. Ask approximately $500 more than your preplanned figure for your trade-in;

3. Tell the salesman if he can get you the deal as you've requested, you're ready to sign the papers.

*(Chapter 6, pages 78-80)*

C. Once in the sales office, remember the following during bargaining:

1. It will take three to four hours;
2. Remain professional always. Never act or get excited or impulsive;
3. "Vacillate" often;
4. Don't be demanding for the first hour or two;
5. Once well into the dealing, begin to make your demands and back them up with the "hard intelligence" figures you've gathered;
6. Offer your down payment in three stages at the appropriate times;
7. Take a pencil, paper and a pocket calculator. And use them;
8. Watch the Worksheet magic;
9. Remember, for every $3.00 increase in what you know your monthly payments should be, the salesman is including roughly $100 more profit;
10. If the dealership will not budge on your trade-in, take it back at the end of the deal;
11. Become a cash buyer in the end.

*(Chapter 6, pages 80-91)*

D. When the contract is prepared, be sure:

1. All figures are correct and in their proper places;
2. No figures are included you did not agree upon;
3. Everything the salesman has promised is shown in writing;
4. The contract is signed by you and the sales manager before leaving the lot.

*(Chapter 7, pages 95-103)*

VI. And finally, if you have not become a cash buyer while in the sales office:

A. Take a copy of the contract to your lender;

B. Get a draft for the total balance owed;

C. Return to the dealership within a day or two and pay off the contract in full.

*(Chapter 9, page 118)*

# CHAPTER NINE

**9**

# DO'S, DON'TS AND
# DEFINITIONS

As was mentioned earlier, it would be impossible to record every situation an artistic buyer might encounter on the lot since some dealerships are, shall we say, highly "creative" when it comes to double-talk and deception. But remember, there's another side to the coin. Your side! The artistic buyer learns quickly to become quite "creative" himself. With this in mind we would like to offer a final list of "Do's and Don'ts," not only for the help they will provide during your next car purchase, but also as a springboard for your imagination. You take it from here and take our word for it, the more "creative" you become, the more fun (and profitable) your own "Car Wars" encounter will be!

1.  **WATCH THE WORKSHEET ACTION—IT'S LIKE MAGIC!**
    This cannot be stressed too much, since the Worksheet the salesman uses prior to drawing up the final contract is the perfect tool for buyer deception. We've included a copy of a typical worksheet on page 116. You'll notice it's divided into four sections: 1) the sale price of the new car; 2) the trade-in; 3) the down payment; and 4) the monthly payments. An

Date: _____

DEMO: _____                     Stock No.: _____

## WORKSHEET
### THIS IS NOT A PURCHASE ORDER

NAME_____

ADDRESS_____

CITY _____ STATE _____

PHONE _____

| year | make | model | cyls. | motor no. | lic. |
|------|------|-------|-------|-----------|------|
|      |      |       |       |           |      |

**BASE PRICE:**

THE SALE PRICE:

| ACCESSORIES:_____ |          |
|--------------------------|----------|
|                          |          |
|                          |          |
|                          |          |
|                          | TOTAL:   |

TRADE-IN

| year | make | model | cyls. | motor no. | lic. |
|------|------|-------|-------|-----------|------|
|      |      |       |       |           |      |

PAYOFF $$$

PAYOFF BANK:

ADDRESS:_____ CITY:_____

TRADE-IN ALLOWANCE $$$$$

| CASH | | PAYMENTS |
|------|------|----------|
| $$$ _____ $$$ _____ | | $$$ _____ |
| Deposit        Dn. Payment | | |

SALESMAN _____ Purchaser's Signature _____

SALES MANAGER _____

accomplished salesman or closer will use each of these sections and the figures they contain virtually like a magician. His sole intent during this part of the dealing process is to juggle, switch, and borrow figures from one section and "quietly" slip them into another section. The end result is the buyer *thinks* he's settled on one amount but in reality it's another (more profitable) figure. Your job (and this is probably the most difficult and critical part of the bargaining process) is to watch, understand and control the amounts in each of the four sections, and to be sure they're really in line with your preplanned figures. As an example, if you are making progress with the new car price, and the salesman has just agreed to lower it by $500, you can bet your bankbook he's going to try to slip $750 quietly into one of the other three sections. He may do it in one lump or a little at a time. And he'll try his best to do it undetected (A skill) by taking your attention off that particular section with a subtle threat, pressure play, comment or talk about another section. Other ways of juggling figures from one section to another are to "accidentally misplace" them, "misunderstand" what you're agreeing to, or make a convenient decimal point error, then hurry you on to talk of another section. The rule of thumb is to remember this: There are countless ways of manipulating *Worksheet dollars* and, if he's a skilled salesman or closer attempting a last ditch effort at squeezing profit into the deal, he'll try them all. Your ways of combating Worksheet "magic" are as follows:

A. Slow or stop the salesman at once when he begins borrowing from one section and adding to another;

B. Have your own worksheet, pencil and calculator on hand and match what he says with what you've got each time he changes sections. A sheet of paper simply divided into four boxes works fine;

C. Always check his math against yours, but later in the deal;

D. Ask for clarification often;

E. Keep an eye and "ear" on all four sections at all times.

Use these techniques and, when the figures are ready to be typed on a contract, verify *again* that each section is correct and you've got it made.

2.  **IF YOU'VE BARGAINED AN EXTREMELY GOOD DEAL, BUT FEEL YOU'VE PUSHED THE DEALERSHIP TO THE LIMIT, *DO* FINANCE THROUGH THEM, THEN PAY THE CONTRACT OFF IN *CASH*, WTHIN A WEEK.**

If you don't mind spending a few more dollars, this is an easier and often more beneficial way to become a cash buyer. It works like this. You allow the dealer to use whatever **APR** he chooses, which, of course, will be high, but bargain for the right *purchase price* and *trade-in equity*, act concerned but not *too* concerned with payments. When you arrive at your preplanned figures (right purchase price and trade-in equity), you then sign the contract as a payment buyer financing through the dealership. Now go immediately to your prearranged lender and borrow the total balance due on the dealership contract (financed amount). Then go back to the dealership, (even on the same day if you wish) and tell them you've decided to pay off the contract in full. All the inflated interest money the salesman had figured into your financing now goes down the drain, and the *most* you are required to pay, if anything, is a minimal contract fee or service charge—usually no more than $25.00. While this may seem a bit underhanded, it is perfectly legal and will say so somewhere on the contract you sign. You should pay the contract off as soon as possible after signing it, though, since once it is processed by the bank the service charges and prepayment penalties could get higher.

3.  **IF AT ALL POSSIBLE, BUY YOUR CAR IN THE MIDDLE OF THE WEEK.**

The majority of cars are sold on weekends(or at end of week). Because of this, dealerships can afford to be more choosy with the deals they close. On the other hand, very few cars are sold on weekdays, simply because most people are working. It is not uncommon, for instance, for a dealership to sell 20 to 30 cars on a weekend but none at *all* between Monday and

Thursday. You can see how "hungry" to sell and much more willing to bend this makes *everyone* in the sales force during the week—including the sales manager!

## 4.   NEVER ALLOW MORE THAN TWO SALESMEN TO ENTER INTO A BARGAINING SESSION.

Some dealerships specialize in breaking down a buyer's defenses through the use of what's known as buyer/salesman turnover. This is done by sending in a series of salesmen, anywhere from two to five (these are often skilled closers and, in some cases, the sales manager himself). Each has his own high pressure techniques. One, for instance, might have the job of convincing you your trade-in is mechanically run-down, and you are being totally unreasonable to ask more than pennies for it. Another may attempt to bully or insult you into paying more for the car you are purchasing than it is worth, or adding accessories. And still another is pressuring you for more down payment money while making you feel cheap or guilty if you don't come across with it. The effect this type of treatment has on the buyer is often devastating. He first becomes confused (who wouldn't?) and then feels totally helpless. Finally he begins to actually *believe* the salesmen and eventually gives up just to get the whole thing over with. If you run into this type of treatment, don't try to fight it. Simply get up and leave at once. Then scratch that car and that dealership off your list—for good. And by all means, let your friends —— where *not* to go when in the market for a car.

## 5.   IF THE DEALERSHIP WILL NOT GIVE YOU CLOSE TO A FAIR PRICE FOR YOUR TRADE-IN, TAKE IT BACK AT THE END OF THE DEAL.

This can save you quite a bit of money if you don't mind selling your car on your own. Let's say you know your trade-in to be worth $2,000 wholesale, but the most the dealership will give you is $600. They *will*, however, sell you *their* car at the preplanned figure you've come up with. During the deal imply you will settle for the $600 for your trade-in, but when the final contract is being prepared simply change your mind. Request that the salesman just add the extra $600 into the total price of the car and forget about the trade-in—you've decided to sell it yourself. You end up by paying $600 more for the car you purchase but make back this amount plus an extra $1,500 when you sell your trade-in to a private party not for the $2,000 *wholesale* figure, but a more reasonable *retail* price of $2500.

## 6. DON'T EXPECT TO CAPTURE A ROCK-BOTTOM BARGAIN FOR HIGH DEMAND, LOW-AVAILABILTY CARS.

The gas crunches we've recently experienced are a prime example of what's known in the car sales business as "seasonal" demands. During these "seasons" (which are these days be coming year round) some of the top selling economy cars sell so fast that the manufacturer simply cannot produce them fast enough or doesn't want to. When this happens, the dealerships can charge, and usually get, outrageously high prices for them. And since they often have a waiting list for those makes and models, they have no reason to even consider bargaining for a lower price. If one of these is the type of car you feel you must have, though, there are several ways you can go. First, you can become an ad buyer; (explained later in this chapter). Second, if you buy the car used—a year or two old—you stand a better chance of getting a fairly good deal. Third, look for a private party sale. These can often produce excellent deals! And finally, discover the skills in this book to its highest level; practice them on several sales teams before attempting to deal with car salesmen selling these high-demand cars. After perfecting your negotiating skills and your ability to waste (consume) time with salesmen, the sales teams' will be "forced" to sell their products because they answer to a higher source—their boss's **boss!** Remember, money is power. Consumers have money.

## 7. IF YOU STILL OWE MONEY ON YOUR TRADE-IN, KNOW THE PAYOFF TO THE DOLLAR.

It is not unusual for an unprepared buyer to walk out of a dealership having traded in his car but still owing money on it! This happens when the buyer hasn't *bothered* to check with whoever originally financed the car to find out what the *exact* payoff is. The salesman first convinces him its worth is minimal and double-talks him into believing the payoff is "probably" a lower figure. The buyer is led to believe that once he trades it in, he's free and clear of the debt. As an example, if you owe $2,000 on your trade-in, and you only get $800 from the dealership, there's still $1200 left owed to the original financer. And just because the pink slip and car keys have changed hands, this doesn't necessarily mean the bill has—no matter what the salesman says. *You* could still owe the remaining $1200. Again, to be a confident and effective bargainer, you must be aware of *all* dollar figures and *exactly* what effect they have on the deal.

## 8. USED CAR CAUTION.

If it's a used car you're in the market for, you'll be able to handle the deal exactly as with a new car but with a single word of *extra* caution. Be sure to give the car a thorough mechanical inspection before you buy. If you are unable to do this yourself, there are a number of articles and pamphlets listed later in this chapter that can aid you. Another means is to test drive the car and take it to a trusted friend or mechanic for a thorough once over. Better yet, why not make your third baseman a mechanic friend? The reasons for this is simply that unlike new cars, used cars are seldom covered by any kind of "warranty." If they are, it's often a very *limited* one and even though you may have made sure to have all repairs put in writing on the contract, once you've bargained an exceptional deal, it may *still* be like pulling teeth to get those repairs done.

## 9. NEVER HAND OVER THE PINK SLIP TO YOUR TRADE-IN OR THE KEYS UNTIL THE CONTRACT IS SIGNED.

The pink slip is the certificate of ownership of your trade-in. Once you've signed your name to the back of it, it no longer belongs to you. You can see what kind of predicament this puts you in if you sign it over simply on the salesman's word that you will get "X" number of dollars for it and later in the deal he decides *you* will simply have to accept less. It's rather awkward to be put in the position of having to bargain for a trade-in you no longer *own!* It's a good idea, by the way,to to keep the pink slip in your wallet during a car purchase. And the keys? It's perfectly all right to let the salesman have them long enough to test drive your car or start the engine when he's checking it out, but get them back immediately afterwards and without exception *before* the real deal begins. Some dealerships have been known to actually "misplace" a buyer's keys (take an extra set) and/or pink slip, as a means of keeping him or her "imprisoned" in the sales office, while being turned over to one salesman or closer after another. Should you inadvertantly find yourself in this position, however, don't be bullied. Stop everything at once and demand your keys or threaten to call the police and notify the Better Business Bureau. Then, when you get them, leave at once.

## 10. IF POSSIBLE, BUY AT THE END OF THE MONTH AND/OR THE END OF THE YEAR AND AT THE DINNER HOUR.

New car dealerships have one sales contest after another, usually on a monthly and yearly basis. The month's top salesman may get anything from a $100 bonus to a paid weekend holiday. As the last days of the month approach, this has an effect on every salesman on the lot. Those on top want to stay there and win the prize. Those close to the top still have a chance of winning it and those on the bottom of the list must (if they are to remain employed) move up. In other words, everyone is more apt to bend in favor of the buyer. You should attempt to buy at the end of the year for the same reason and a few others. Once the year in which a car is manufactured elapses, several things happen to make a car very costly for the dealership to keep around. First, as far as the banks, credit unions and other lenders are concerned, it becomes not a new but a *used* car even if it has zero miles on it. This means they will lend smaller amounts of money for its purchase, which in turn makes it harder for the dealership to sell. Also, the car depreciates (loses value) substantially and the dealership must either sell it fast or absorb the loss themselves. If you plan to keep the car for 7 to 10 years, this immediate depreciation won't hurt you. If, on the other hand, you trade-in and buy a new car every year or so, you should stay away from last year's models. And, finally, dealerships do, as they advertise, simply want to get the old ones off the lot to make way for the brand new (more profitable) ones.

Buying at the dinner hour can sometimes offer you still another advantage. In some cases the closers and sales managers leave the lot to have dinner. The fairly new salesmen may be left "holding down the fort" until the heavies get back!

## 11.   IF POSSIBLE, BUY AROUND CHRISTMAS TIME.

If you stop to think about it, this puts almost all the odds in your favor. It's the end of the year, the end of the month, and in addition, it's a lean time of the year for car sales, since most people are too financially strapped after Christmas shopping to even think about buying a car! This lean time, incidentally, usually continues into the early months of the next year—until tax refunds begin to come in! So, if you miss the end of the year, your chances are still fairly good until about March.

### DEFINTIONS

The following "treasury" of dealership terms may offer some additional insight into their structure and workings. A note of caution, though, don't purposely use any of this *jargon* to *impress* the salesman with how much you know about the business. You will end up doing exactly that. This will tend to both anger and place him on guard. And it may just prompt him to enlist the help of a highly skilled closer early in the deal!

## 1.   TURNOVER (T.O.) HOUSE

A car lot or dealership in which the salesman's job is simply to excite the buyer with unconfirmed promises, get him or her through the test ride and into the sales office. At this point the buyer is "turned over" to one or several closers whose job it is to systematically take away the "promises" previously made and write up the *most* profitable deal possible.

## 2.  STRAIGHT SELL HOUSE

A car lot or dealership where the original salesman is allowed, in most cases, to carry the entire deal from start to finish.

## 3.  ARTISTIC "AD BUYER"

A buyer who, having gathered soft and hard intelligence, arranges for outside financing in advance, then watches the car ads in local newspapers for what he or she *knows* to be wholesale (zero-profit) deals. Then, when the type of car they are in the market for is advertised, they rush to the lot when it opens its doors and demand that car for the advertised price, in an across-the-board, cash deal. Remember, the intent of wholesale ad cars is simply to get the buyer *onto* the lot so a salesman can then steer him toward more profitable deals. If the buyer sticks to his guns, however, the dealership, by law, *must* sell the car for the advertised price. Most ad cars, incidentally, are made available on Friday mornings—so be ready!

## 4.  LOWBALL

An offer (a massive discount on new car) impossible to produce, on which the salesman has made on the lot, to you, in an attempt to get you into the sales office. A "lowball" is also intended to bring you back to his lot after you've shopped around since no other lot will be able to beat it.

## 5.  HIGHBALL

Opposite of lowball. And extremely *high* offer on your trade-in, equally as impossible to produce, and with the same intent as the lowball.

## 6.  BOOK

The wholesale value of a trade-in or used car, according to the current *Kelly Bluebook*. Lending institutions use the *Bluebook* as a reference base for amounts financed. Dealerships use it as aid in figuring trade-in profit.

### 7. BIRD DOGGER

A third party who refers a buyer to a particular salesman, and in return receives a small "bird dogger's" fee—if the sales man makes the sale.

### 8. SWITCH

The act of changing something in the deal, resulting in a higher profit. It could be "switching" the buyer from a low profit car to a more profitable car, adding accessories, reducing trade-in equity, "switching" figures on a worksheet, or switching strategies once a particular buyer's weaknesses become apparent.

### 9. SHOCK TREATMENT

Shocking the buyer, thus intimidating and weakening him by quoting some unexpected figure. This is usually done with an intimidating stare and at some unexpected place in the bargaining session. An example might be, "Okay, Mr. Smith, let's see. Now, the banks require one fourth down, that will be $2,000. Will that be cash or check? . . ."

### 10. CASH BUYER

A buyer who deals in cash only and lets the dealership know it from the start. He often carries several $100 bills on him to impress the salesman and clinch the deal. He usually returns within a few days with a bank draft or check to pay off the contract.

### 11. DIFFERENCE BUYER

A buyer who deals in one figure only: the difference between his trade-in and the cash price of the car. Example: A car with your preplanned profit *already* figured in it, is worth $8,000 and you hope to get $3,000 for your trade-in—the difference, a $5,000 bottom line sale price, *is* the figure you are bargaining for.

### 12. PAYMENT BUYER

A buyer who is financing through the dealership's bank.

### 13. LOOKER

A person who visits car lots irritating the salesman by taking up his time with no real *intention* of buying a car.

## 14. SHOPPER

A qualified buyer in the shopping stage. One who, if handled properly, can and will buy today.

## 15. BUYER

A person who is definitely ready and financially qualified to buy today. If he is a "typical buyer," the salesman need only excite him by dangling the *right* "carrots" at the *right* time!

## 16. THE LUNCH BRIGADE

Groups of "lookers" who spend their lunch hours browsing in car lots. Since they, like individual "lookers," have no intention of buying, they are also irritants to the salesmen.

## 17. APPRAISAL

While this may be given verbally, it is often a slip of paper with a *tentative* value of the buyer's trade-in written on it by the salas manager. Note: If it is set off by a star, asterisk or some othar external marking, this often means the sales manager is letting the salesman know he can go several hundred dollars higher if the buyer demands it. So demand it!

## WORKSHEET/CONTRACT DEFINITIONS

## 1. THE FULL PRICE OF THE CAR

No matter what type of buyer you are , this figure should be the *full and complete* price of the car you have agreed on. If you are strictly a cash buyer, without a trade-in, it is the only figure you need concern yourself with.

## 2. TRADE-IN EQUITY

If you are a difference or a payment buyer, this figure would be the *exact* and total price the dealership has agreed to pay you for your trade-in.

## 3. DOWN PAYMENT

If you are a payment buyer, this should be the *exact* and total figure you've agreed to pay, in cash, as a down payment.

### 4. PAYMENTS

If you are a payments buyer this should be the *exact* and total figure you've been quoted as your monthly payments.

### 5. CONTRACT LENGTH

This should be the full time period during which you've agreed to borrow the money; *e.g.*, 36 months, 48 months, etc.

### 6. FINANCE CHARGES

If you are a payments buyer, this is the fee the dealership charges to carry their financing. While it can sometimes add up to a sizable sum, provided all the other figures you agreed upon are accurate *(especially monthly payments)* you need not be concerned with it (except when you let dealership finance your loan).

### 7. APR

If you are a payments buyer, this is the *true* annual percentage rate you are being charged by the dealership to borrow the money.

### 8. AMOUNT FINANCED

If you are a payments buyer, this figure should be the *exact* difference between your down payment, plus your agreed trade-in equity, and the full and complete price of the car you are purchasing.


## SUGGESTED READING

In the task of revising this book, to my surprise, I found few articles as informative as the below listed. Visit your local library and glance through them. They will assist you in gathering your soft and hard intelligence. Also, the reference librarian will show you where the pamphlets are located on this subject.

Your visit in the library will be worth the time invested.[5*]

---

[5*]  Don't forget to glance over several copies of Changing Times (Dec issues) and Consumer Reports (April issues) on display in the periodical section of the library. These magazines provide an invaluable service for their readers.

1. How to buy a new car and sell your old one:
   *Motor Trend*, pp. 43-47, May 1975

2. Knocking down the sticker price on a new car:
   *Changing Times*, pp. 11-13, October 1975

3. Dealing with the dealer:
   *Consumer Reports*, pp. 192-3, April 1976

4. Making the deal: old rules in a new ball game:
   *Consumer Reports*, pp. 298-302, April 1974

5. King of the iron merchants:
   *Motor Trend*, pp. 54-57, December 1975

6. Have I got a deal for you!
   *Motor Trend*, pp. 77-81 July 1976

7. The Gray Market: Cheaper but chancy imports: Changing
   Times, pp. 55-59, Nov 1985.

**Free Publications**

Consumer Infornnation Center
Pueblo, Colorado 81009

- General catalog listing available publications:
- Common Sense in Buying a Safe Used Car
- Shopping for Credit Can Save You Cash
- Common Sense in Buying a New Car

Mr. John Finsland
Shell Oil Company
P.O. Box 61609
Houston, Texas 77208

- Please send me answer book No. 4, "The Car
  Buying and Selling Book."

**Fee**

Council of Better Business Bureaus, Inc.
1150 17th St.
N.W., Washington, D.C. 20036

Please send costs of below publications (about 5¢ each):
- Tips on Sales Contracts: Pub. No. 208

- How to Buy New Cars
- Tips on Buying a Used Car: Pub. No. 311-02247
- Tips on Renting a Car: Pub. No. 244

Superintendent of Documents
U.S. Government Printing Office
Washington, D.C. 20402

- Please send "Automobiles Imported into the U.S.."
- General Catalog List

Further information is available in your local library. Ask the librarian where they keep the Reader's Guide Index and consumer pamphlets filed.

I strongly recommend this "How To" book on negotiating, a tradeback book published in 1980 by *Citadel* Press called, "You can Negotiate Anything," by Herb Cohen ($5.95). a classic example of negotiating skills available to anyone who dares to learn them. I salute this author's efforts in presenting these negotiating—skills to the public. The user of this book will discover (or rediscover) the power of time & money.

A final point. I would like to repeat that the picture painted of the car salesman and the dealership in this little melodrama was hardly a pretty one. I've chosen to paint it in that way simply to prepare you for the worst you may encounter. And while the "worst," in many instances, has proven to be the rule rather than the exception, remember, it's not always the case. Some salesmen and dealerships will treat you as honestly as they claim and still take enormous profits off the average consumer. This is as it should be, since it is a car salesman's job to be persuasive and indeed, his only means of survival in a tough and competitive business. Neither he nor the dealership can be criticized for simply doing a good, honest job. Dishonesty, on the other hand, is not a salesman's job. As an *artistic* buyer you will be able to recognize the difference between the two and deal with each accordingly. In doing so, both you and the salesman (especially the honest ones) will come away from the deal you have made with a sense of mutual respect—you respecting his persuasive ability and he respecting your ability to bargain "with the best of them." And that is what an *artistic* car buy is all about . . . .

# 10

# THE ARTISTIC BUYER'S
# READINESS TEST

You should now be fully prepared to enter the world of retail
auto sales as an artistic buyer. Just in case there is any doubt
in your mind, however, the following test has been provided
to either verify or remove your doubt—forever. Here's how
it works. You will be given ten typical car lot situations in
which something may or may *not* be right. Following each are
a few related questions. Read each thoroughly and jot on a
piece of paper what you, as an artistic buyer, feel is right or
wrong and what you would or would not have done in each
of the situations. The answers begin on page 140 and obviously
yours don't have to match word for word. Following each answer
is the chapter or chapters you may care to refer to which discusses
this situation. Scoring? All ten right makes you a veritable Van
Gogh among artistic buyers. Nine is good and . . . eight is,
well, . . ., "so-so." Anything below six and you had better do
a bit of re-reading before attempting to buy your next car.
Good luck and . . . good bargaining!

**SITUATION NO. 1:**

You have completed your buyer's plan of action and are
ready to go back to the lot and make your deal. Glancing through
the morning paper, however, you find a special advertised on

a different lot. It is *exactly* the car you want, but a different color. The advertised price you know is *wholesale*, and for that you feel you can live without the original color you had planned on. You rush down to the lot and inquire about the special to one of the salesmen. Your conversation goes something like this:

**Salesman:** Hi, I'm Tom Jones. Can I help you?

**You:** Yes, I'd like to see the special you advertised this morning (you show the salesman the newspaper ad).

**Salesman:** Gee, I believe we just sold that one. We do have another special, though. A car just about like that one—actually a better car—it's a few more bucks but those specials are never really good cars. It's right over here (the salesman begins to walk in that direction saying), if I could get you the same kind of deal on it, would you be interested in buying today?

## QUESTION:

What is the salesman attempting to do?
How should you respond?

## SITUATION NO. 2:

You have followed the buyer's art to the letter and just closed what you know to be an excellent deal. You have just switched over to a cash buyer and the contract is now being prepared. As the salesman is writing it up, however, you happen to notice a figure which doesn't look like one you had discussed. The following conversation follows:

**You:** What's that $400 figure?

**Salesman:** That's our standard five year warranty policy. We write it in on all contracts, for your protection. There's no charge to you, though, if you don't want it, we'll just initial the cancel clause. You know, ma'am, we agreed on this $1,000 down payment, but it looks like I'm going to need more to get those $272 a month

134

payments I promised you. Do you have more down payment available, ma'am? Let's see, I'd need . . . about . . . Can you give me $300 more?

## QUESTION:

Is this contract session going as it should?
If not, why?
How should the artistic buyer now respond?

## SITUATION NO. 3:

In the midst of your trade-in talk, your salesman excuses himself for a moment to run a few figures by his boss. Moments later another salesman enters. He introduces himself, says your original salesman got an important phone call and has asked him to help you in the meantime. He's polite enough at first, but soon begins to infer that you should literally be "ashamed" of yourself for asking that kind of money for an obviously mistreated, mechanically defective car like *yours*. As you begin defending your position, he abruptly cuts you off and says he'll need to see your pink slip. You hand it over, and after grumbling a bit he gets to his feet. He says he's got to verify the engine ID number and excuses himself. In a few moments still another salesman enters. After his introduction, he says he's just gotten a call from the finance department and your credit rating is questionable. As a result, more down payment will be required and since everyone has agreed that trade-in of yours is only worth a fraction of what you asked, he'll have to increase the new car price to offset this figure.

## QUESTION:

Is this bargaining session going okay?
If not, why?
What should you do at this point?

## SITUATION NO. 4:

You are in the sales office and bargaining well for what you know is an excellent deal. The salesman has actually been extremely pleasant about it all and seems totally sincere in the points he has made. The deal is now getting close and you are making a play for a $2,000 figure for your trade-in (you actually know this to be a little high).

**You:** I'm afraid I have to have $2,000 for my trade-in, at least. I saw one the other day, in terrible shape, and the party was asking $2,800 for it.

**Salesman:** Okay, listen, I'll get you the $ 2,000. It's high, but I've got to sell this deal and if that's what it takes, okay. (He now writes $2,000 in large black numbers on his worksheet in the space provided for trade-in allowance.) You do have the pink slip here today, I assume?

**You:** Yes, I do.

**Salesman:** (Handing you a pen.) Fine, now if you'll just sign it on the back to confirm that, we'll get on to the financing I mentioned . . . .

## QUESTION:
What is the salesman attempting to do and why?
What should you do?
Or say?

## SITUATION NO. 5:
After four hours of hard bargaining, during which time the salesman has been extremely crafty, you have managed to close an excellent deal and get an accurate contract written up. Feeling proud of yourself, you are now writing out the down payment check for $1,600. When you have it completed the following conversation ensues:

**Salesman:** Fine. Now I'll just have to confirm the check (he now picks up the phone, dials a few numbers), "Hi, Joe, this is Al. Listen, I have a check—a down for $1,600—and we've closed the deal, can I . . . Oh . . . okay, sure. He won't mind a ten day free trial in a brand new car. Hell, who wouldn't?!! (He then hangs up the phone.) We'll have to let the check go through, first, sir. It should take three to five days. I'll just verify the final contract with the bank and you can go ahead and take the car home for a week or ten days at no charge. Once the check clears and your loan papers go through, I'll give you a buzz so you can come back in and sign the contract. Here's the keys to *your* brand new car . . . .

## QUESTION:

What should you do and/or say now?
What is the salesman attempting to do?
And what is likely to happen in a week or ten days?

## SITUATION NO. 6:

You have been successfully bargaining with a salesman who went to get the boss' approval on your current offer. In his place a closer has returned. His position, of course, is that the dealership simply must have more money.

**Salesman:** Ma'am, I'm being perfectly honest with you. I mean it. This isn't the type of dealership that believes in mistreating customers. In fact, I'm going to prove it. (He now takes an official looking tag from his file. The tag reads: "$10,000—wholesale." The suggested retail sticker, however, said $11,500 and you were told by your bank the car was worth $9,000 wholesale.) This is the receipt we had to sign to get that car, ma'am. Now, we need $11,000 and you're asking us to sell it to you for $9,500!! We'd be losing $1,500 bucks."

## QUESTION:

What is the salesman attempting to do?
What should you do?
Or say?

## SITUATION NO. 7:

You are out gathering your hard intelligence. At the first two lots you visited you found nothing you liked, but now at the third one you've found exactly the car you wanted. And what's more, the salesman is brand new and willing to let it go cheap. On top of that, he's offered you $500 *more* than you know your trade-in is worth! The only problem is he's going on vacation tomorrow and he knows for a fact none of the other salesmen (all old pros) would even *think* about making you a deal like that, so you've got to go into his office and write it up now . . . .

**QUESTION:**

What is the salesman attempting to do?
What should you do?

## SITUATION NO. 8:

Having completed your buyers plan, you have called the lot back to contact the salesman you will deal with. You are told, however, he no longer works there. After thinking this over, you decide to simply go back and try to get another new salesman, if possible. When you get to the lot and find a salesman, you ask about the car in question and are told he's sorry, but that one just sold. He does happen to have one *exactly* like it, though, and he can get you a discount on it if you feel you'd like to buy it today.

**QUESTION:**

Should you look at the car he is suggesting?
Should you consider buying it today?

## SITUATION NO. 9:

It is Saturday morning at 10:00 a.m. on May 3rd, and you have returned to the lot to put your buyer's plan into action and get an excellent deal. The salesman seems impatient, though, and unwilling to budge more than a few dollars. After a half an hour of futile bargaining you, too, are getting impatient and you've got an appointment to meet a friend at 12 for lunch, which reminds you—you're getting hungry. Finally, you decide to play all your cards and get it over with. You do exactly that and the salesman tells you he's sorry but there's no way he can accept your offer. He then gives you *his* final offer and tells you he's busy. If you'd care to buy the car at his figures, he'll write it up. If not, there are other customers waiting outside . . . . Since you've gone to this much trouble you decide to just get it over with and buy at the figures he's demanding.

## QUESTION:

Was this an artistic buy?
If not, what did the buyer do wrong?
Should he have gone ahead with the buy?

## SITUATION NO. 10:

You've entered the sales office and the salesman has writ ten up your tentative offer on his worksheet. The four figures you've proposed are: New car price—$9,500; trade-in equity-$2,000; down payment—$1,500; and payments—$250.00. As the salesman now begins to figure on his adding machine, and at the same time do addition on the worksheet, his conversation speeds up:

**Salesman:** Let's see. $1,500 down—sir, I'm not sure if the boss'll buy that or not. But, okay, now, $2,000 trade-in against that $1,500 and $250. Right, $1,750 here and $8.000—sir, I really don't know . . .

**You:** (Looking at his worksheet and your own.) Wait a minute, I . . .

**Salesman:** I mean, he'll probably throw me out of the office, sir. I'll need another $500 at least. Can you manage $500 more down?

**You:** Well, ah... no, I can't, but . . .

**Salesman:** Okay, well, we'll go with it and see what develops. Now, gee, that $2,000 trade-in from $9,500 leaves a financed amount of $8,500. By the way, did you say you wanted those tinted windows or not? I'll tell you, at $350 they're a bargain.

**You:** No, I don't, but just a minute. You've got some mistakes there.

**Salesman:** (with an intimidating stare:) Sir, believe me, I do this every day. Take my word for it, the figures will all come out right. Okay, now. What did we say? Oh, yeah. $350. Now I'll just . . .

## QUESTION:

What is the salesman attempting to do?
What are his "mistakes?
What should you do?

---

## RESPONSE NO. 1:

An artistic buyer would realize when the salesman said, "I believe we sold that one," he didn't commit himself one way or the other. What he did try to do, obviously, was to use the lot and a vague, "If I could . . . would you buy today" to steer you toward a profitable rather than a wholesale deal. You would respond by telling the salesman the sale car was *exactly* what you had in mind, and further, you would like to know for *sure* whether it was sold or not. If it has been sold, you would have said good day and returned to your original plan. If not, you would know you've got him over a barrel. Having advertised the car at a wholesale price, he has no choice but to sell it for that price. Remember, however, we will still try his darndest, all the way through the deal, to change your mind. (See Chapters 4 and 8.)

## RESPONSE NO. 2:

You should respond by stopping the deal immediately and not continuing until you fully understand this $400 figure. Also, standard or not, it should not appear on your contract since you did not discuss a warranty. Therefore, you should also have it removed. No, this session is not going as it should, since the salesman is attempting to slip an extra $400 into the deal and change the subject by *crossing* you over to payments talk rather than explaining the issue at hand. (See Chapter 6.)

## RESPONSE NO. 3:

Going okay? On the contrary, you've gotten yourself into trouble. You've obviously run into a high pressure turnover house and are letting yourself be bullied and slowly "persuaded" to "cough-up" what the dealership wants or else. You made a major mistake by letting the last salesman take your pink slip, since it may now be "misplaced" and used as a tool to keep you in your *seat* until the dealership has succeeded in *pressuring* you into a buy. What should you do? Get to your feet immediately and demand that your pink slip is returned to you at once or you will walk to the nearest phone and call both the police and the Better Business Bureau. Once the pink slip is produced, you should leave immediately—that is, unless you care to stick around just long enough to do a little insulting of your own! (See Chapter 9.)

## RESPONSE NO. 4:

He is attempting to get you to sign away your trade-in before a binding contract has been written. You should say that you will be *more* than happy to sign and confirm the transaction once the contract is signed—and only then.

## RESPONSE NO. 5:

You should say you don't care to take the car and leave the contract. You should also tell the salesman the check is perfectly good and he's welcome to call your bank right now to confirm that. The salesman is attempting to get your down payment check *without* having sold you a thing since no contract has been signed. And in three to five days? You'll get the call, all right, and be asked to come in and sign the contract. There's a good chance, however, it will not be the same contract, but a different one involving *more* money because there were problems getting your loan papers through, or any number of "unfortunate" reasons. And your check? Cashed, cleared, and . . . gone! (See Chapter 8.)

## RESPONSE NO. 6:

No matter how official it may look, the so called receipt can not be legitimate with such a little profit margin. The salesman is attempting to convince you with a so called "receipt" he is losing *money* on your deal. And what should you do?

Level with him. Tell him he's trying to deceive you and you know it, since you were told the wholesale price of the car by your bank, and it's $9,000. And also mention that if a bank is going to lend money on cars, there's no way they're going to be close to $2,000 *misinformed* on the price of one. And finally, with your offer of $9,500, they're not by any means losing money, they're making a fast $500, which as far as you're concerned, is plenty of profit. (See Chapters 3 and 8.)

**RESPONSE NO. 7:**

The salesman is obviously trying to "highball" you, in an attempt to get you into his office unprepared and thinking impulsively. You should ask for his card and tell him you'd like to shop some more. If you do decide to buy this car, you'll just wait a week since you're in no *rush,* and then get in touch with him. Then you should be on your way! (See Chapters 4 and 8.)

**RESPONSE NO. 8:**

Why not have a look at it? If it does turn out to be *exactly* like the other one, it is still what you want. As far as considering buying it today, that depends. If it *is* the same make and model with the same extras, yes, you can consider buying today, since the figures you've arrived at are based on those three criteria. If any of those things are different, though, you should not consider entering the sales office until you've had a chance to get the new figures you need and modify your plan to include them. (See Chapters 3, 4 and 5.)

**RESPONSE NO. 9:**

An artistic buy? Disastrous is a better word. The list of wrongs goes something like this. He or she shouldn't have bought at 10:00 a.m., shouldn't have had an appointment with a friend at 12:00, shouldn't have gotten hungry and shouldn't have played all the cards so soon! As far as going ahead with the deal, sure, why not? This buyer would never make an artist anyway . . . . (See Chapters 5 and 8.)

## RESPONSE NO. 10:

This salesman is attempting to work a little "magic" on his worksheet, while at the same time keeping your attention on other worksheet sections. His "mistakes"? Ah, yes. Well, he's already managed to make your down payment $1,750 instead of $1,500 by "mistakenly" adding your payments figure into it. And he's quoted a financed amount of $8,500, which is incorrect. Along with your trade-in equity, your *down payment* should also have been deducted from the new car price. The real financed amount at this point should be $6,000. And who knows *what* he's planned to do with the $350 figure he's tossing around for the tinted windows! Your defense? Stop him immediately. Refuse to talk about another point until you've verified what he has in each of the four worksheet sections coincided with your figures. If everything matches, fine. If not, politely, but firmly, correct his "errors" before proceeding.

# CHAPTER ELEVEN

# THE EARLY DAYS OF A NEW CAR SALESMAN

## BASIC TRAINING

Purpose: To understand the point of view of the sales team's generals, lieutenants, the front line troops, and their required duties in the battle of wits to capture the maximum amount of dollars from the marketplace. Their success is only limited by their selling skills. Once you understand the functions of the members of that sales team and their roles in the dealership, you (the buyer) should have all the ammunition you'll need to encounter even the most "aggressive" salesman on the lot. Remember, while the sales team practices their techniques several times a **DAY,** the car buyer, goes through this exercise only a few times in his/her *lifetime!* Practice will, prepare you against most of the sales teams' assaults!

Everyone knows what it takes to become a car salesman. Take one flashy sports coat, add tie, white belt, patent leather shoes and, of course, a gaudy pinky ring—and there you are! Well—almost. Besides a gift-of-gab, you must also now learn and perfect many other skills before you can expect to survive this **HIGHLY** competitive world. You must learn to *sell* cars, not just talk about them with prospective buyers. It's going to be tough to survive this treacherous "training period."

But to do so will bring you heaps of pride in your quest to please your general and you'll try even *harder* to please your general (manager) to stay employed.

For now let's forget the manufacturer's specifications to these automobiles. We'll concentrate on how to capture prospective buyers and convert them into **"NOW"** buyers. Your goal will be **TO SELL** cars at **MAXIMUM PROFIT** off this lot **TODAY!** but to do this, you must discover the buyers' desires and weaknesses. You must learn how to control him and lead him through a special maze of selling rituals. You're not alone— the sales team will be backing you up all the way—you can't lose! Remember, the sales team **ALWAYS** takes maximum profit. After all—that's as American as apple pie. Spend this time learning the basic "selling rules" and "strategies" and you will discover the consumer is really no competition at all. The "better player" always wins! Practicing everyday, you'll become the *expert* at selling cars—how can you possibly loose?

Some of these "selling rules" you'll need to master are:

> That every **SALE** be a profitable one;
> **Sell** your car with a team spirit;
> Strive to sell any car on the lot - **TODAY!**;
> Maintain a business-like image;
> Exude confidence, appear successful.

So, now, let's pretend in this chapter that you the reader are entertaining the idea of becoming a real, live car salesman— a brand spanking **"NEW"** car salesman! Where do you begin, what do you need to know, how can you prepare to "perform" for your new employer? What do you need to do to **STAY** employed?

Let's follow one enterprising young man during his first few days on the job. He's just beginning, so we'll call him a "private." He's going to be in the front-line assault and he must also answer to a "chain of command."

His immediate superior will probably be a more seasoned trooper, we'll call him a "lieutenant." This lieutenant will work together with our private on the front lines to "capture" as many consumers as they can for the dealership's sake. The "General" is the sales manager (new or used sales manager), He and the lieutenant will have many anxious moments over the effectiveness of our "new" private. Fewer than 10% of these raw recruits hired will survive the first year.

We'll name our private Mr. Clark. The young salesman's **boss** or lieutenant we'll call Mr. Roberts and the sales manager or general we'll tag Mr. Patten. As we unfold our little scenario, we see our players armed with a selling scheme *laced* with pitches and plays to assure *maximum* profit-taking in the marketplace all ready to do their best against any unwary consumer who might dare enter their territory—the car lot.

The general is busy most of the time. He hired this new trooper, Mr. Clark and now rushes him to the front lines (a strategic location on the car lot). Mr. Clark is assigned to Mr Roberts an aggressive lieutenant platoon leader of 4 other car salesmen on the lot. Immediately he takes Mr. Clark for a familiarization tour of his post. And assigns him to special duties as a "beginner" salesman.

**Lieutenant**
**Roberts:**  "Son, the first few weeks can be very tough for you. I'm here to teach you the basics. Let me suggest that you plan your attack—er I mean conversations with the car buyers. Capture them, hold their interest. Only say enough to maintain buyer-control."

**Private Clark:**  "What's buyer-control?"

**Lieutenant**
**Roberts:**  "Buyer-control is a *phenomenon* by which consumers will react to your sales pitches—and will follow you around until you're ready to take them into your office to complete the sale."

**Private Clark:**  "Well, what do I do then?"

**Lieutenant**
**Roberts:**  "Well, do not worry, the sales team will take these *controlled* buyers and *finalize* the sale. Team work takes maximum $s! But this all

149

takes time, so make sure you start off right by being in the right place to capture the "real" car buyers. Remember, most of the people you contact will fail to qualify. They won't be ready to buy today. The sales team recognizes this and tries to convert as many shoppers as possible into real live "now" buyers.

"Learn to qualify your buyers. Ask questions. Do they have a savings account? Are they employed? Do you think they can be excited into buying today?

"Above all, avoid any horse-trading! Let the sales team (lieutenants) do this for you! You just say anything you must to get your buyers into one of those sales offices. Just be a "greeter" and "tickle" their ears!

"It's a difficult task to sell a car today, so practice. Practice makes perfect is an axiomatic rule—remember it!

"So now, let's get going, this is basic training! Approach as many potential buyers as you can—be aggressive and practice, practice, practice. Do this and you'll automatically do well."

At this point, let's get some rules and role playing straight! It's Mr. Clark's job to set the tone of bargaining. It's going to be Mr. Roberts' job to "save the deal" by offering counter offers and better prices to the customers.

The two sellers are setting inside one of the sales offices practicing some role playing acts. Mr. clark begins his selling "act" with Mr. Robert as the buyer. Mr. Clark starts by indicating a low trade-in figure —emotions fly— Mr. Roberts retorts, with Mr. Clark red-faced and in shock trying to counter to save the deal.

**Lieutenant Roberts:**    "Well—now let's look at this again! (As the customer cools down, they start talking about their "beautiful, old faithful car" that they have reluctantly decided to use as the "trade-in." They do so with renewed hope that they might possibly talk the salesman into a higher price for the car.)

"Allright, I think I can raise the trade-in $100.00"

Mr. Clark moves quickly to do just that—but then the customer's emotions and questions start to mount. Mr. Clark quickly shifts the focus to the new car price, but with yet no set figure on the trade-in.

The new car sells for $$$. Now the consumer demands a discount. Mr. Clark, as coached by Mr. Roberts, counters with only $100.00 discount and states that as a brand *new* car salesman, he's not authorized to give discounts. But he assures the customer that he's on their side! Mr. Roberts is amazed at this new salesman's *creativeness* at selling.

Now, as before, Mr. Clark moves on quickly, without getting bogged down in details. After all tying the details down is Mr. Roberts job.

Next comes the down payment section. Mr. Clark demands 1/3 down in cash—strickly for "good faith," you understand!

**Private Clark:** Whispers to his leader, "It'll take that much cash for some "holding power." (Having taken out the car keys.) Maybe we could temporarily 'lose' these."

The customer starts to weaken. (Mr. Roberts role plays a little weakness)

Mr. Clark seizes the moment and again, without settling any previous points, moves on to the monthly payment section.

Mr. Clark, still following the battle plan laid out for him by Mr. Roberts, indicates to the customer, that a large monthly payment is what his chart indicates (**Secret**: it shows, totals well above the full deal). But he offers them a discount; now the customer *knows* that he's on their side. (really).

**Private Clark:** "Mr. Roberts, what do I do now?"

**Lieutenant
Roberts:**

"Now you call me in for an *O.K.* and I'll do the rest. It's my job to repeat all your steps on the trade-in, the price of the new car, the down payment, the monthly payments, but it's up to me to tell the customer what it really takes to buy a car today. In other words, Mr. Clark, you start the shock treatment and I repeat it over and over until the customer weakens. It's at this point that we can get the maximum dollar profit for the dealership.

Tempers may run high in your sales office. Call in someone to assist you in soothing the buyer.

Again, remember this is a team effort! If we can't extract enough profit from the buyer, the General will call in another Lieutenant and another until the maximum profit is assured. Also, during this phase of the deal, your position is to be seated near the sales office door. If any buyer makes an attempt to escape, they'll· have to climb over you. It's just a suggestion.

Situations aren't always this drastic, but the sooner you learn to *control* the buyer, the *sooner* the big money will be made.

Who knows, maybe with practice, you can be a professional in, say, 90-120 days." (Mr. Clark also acknowledges the inference that if he doesn't shape up quickly, he's going to be looking for a new job.)

Let's take a little "time out" from our Private Clark and his basic training course to explain something of the General and his interface with the Lieutenants. All through this selling-process, the General is kept informed of the events transpiring in the sales office. Several Lieutenants constantly honing their skills on what to say, not only to close the sale, but to do so with the maximum profit for the dealership, are always ready. The General may call on any one of them to assist. There is also a natural "pecking order" among the lieutenants and salesmen according to each individual's skills at handling the buyer and at being able to extract as much profit as is possible.

Now let's rejoin Private Clark who is just being approached by another salesman, another team member.

**2nd Salesman:** "Hi Clark, my name is Madonna, did you get the buyer's "big yes" on a contract yet? Let me give you a little sales *secret.*"

**Private Clark:** "What do you mean?"

**2nd Salesman:** "There are several 'yeses' required by the customer before they will consider signing a contract. Get them to say 'yes' a lot and do it right from the beginning of the deal. I talk to the car buyer as if they've already decided to buy. In fact, on the demo ride, I make a safety check of the car with the customers help. They operate all the knobs and switches. They visualize showing it off to their friends. At this point, the buyer has taken the first step to making the car theirs. And, through all this, I've become their ally, fighting to make their dream come true.

"Remember, your commissions are earned only on the cars you sell—all other profits are shared by the sales team's command.

"Oh, oh, here comes the General. I'd better start back to my post! and by the way, this little "trade secret is going to cost you a dinner!

"Oh, and one other thing, if you can capture a trade-in at well below wholesale, let me know. I'll try to sell it to one of my customers. There's tremendous profits to be made in used cars! Good luck Clark. It's easy to sell cars, especially if you are sexy looking."

The general walks his domain, watching his most valued troops, the aggressive salesmen, thrusting and parrying in word battles to capture buyers, to corner them into the sales office and on to total victory and the maximum profits for the team!

**General Patten:** "Mr. Clark, come here! (Recognizing the new salesman who captured his first car buyer and safely delivered him to his Lieutenant and to a final sale.) Where do you think your next car buyer (sale) will enter the dealership?."

Mr. Clark without hesitation points towards a walkway and leaps towards it!

**General Patten:** "Hold on, there, young man—I'm not through with you yet!

"I want to let you know that selling buyers that are ready to buy is not enough! I want you to get me some shoppers, get me some lookers. You must learn how to convert them well. Deal quickly. Find the motive that will turn an impulse buyer into *today's* sale! Get the prospect's attention, increase his interest and desire to buy and buy today! Keep your defenses up. Be ready to thwart responses like I'll think it over, "I can get a better deal at so-and-so dealer" or "I'll have to talk it over with my wife. Let this borderline buyer know that even though you'll hardly make any profit, you'll be willing to help him get the best possible deal **TODAY!** If you leave your buyer believing he's just gotten the greatest deal of a *lifetime,* he'll boast about it to his friends. That means more commissions for *you.* Don't get hung up with how emotional the deal gets inside the sales office; most buyers will forget about that very quickly. But the referral business will keep you in commissions for the rest of your time here at the dealership! Well, you're off to a good start. Mr. Roberts indicates you're learning fast (a must if you expect to make it in this business).

You've got a gift-of-gab, you're acting skills are visable. You stand a good chance of becoming a professional.

"If you feel yourself loosing control of any prospect—call one of your fellow salesmen, or me for **IMMEDIATE** assistance. We work as a team! **Right!**

"Mr. Clark, you'll find that some "roleplaying" is required to do business with todays' consumers. You need not become an actor but we do have "best" car salesman of the month contests for the "aggressive" sellers. So experiment and find your own *niche* here at the dealership.

"I remember one young salesman who hurt himself on a skiing trip. Limping and in great need to contact buyers, he became an instant winner of color TV sets, suits and **BIG DOLLAR** rewards for his creativeness! I guess the consumers felt sympathetic for his injury. Anyway, he still limps, long after his injury healed.

"Discover your own routines and make sure you feel comfortable with them.

"The dealership, *your* fortress, is *your* territory—it's where most of your sales will occur. Only so many buyers will cross into your area. Your goal is to capture these easy buyers. Also, you must convert as many shoppers as you can into now buyers. Shoppers are usually **FAIR** risks to the banking industry. But avoid those lookers, after your training period, they usually have no way to go with the financing institutions. They may be unemployed, have no trade-in nor down payment. Determine their position quickly and don't spend any more time with them than you absolutely have to! Then transfer them to one of the weaker salesmen

on the team for practice. Who knows maybe
a sale will be made."

Mr. Clark rushes over to his Boss and reports for further
instructions for the day.

**Private Clark:** "What's a looker?"

**Lieutenant
Roberts:**

"They could be people who are too young and
need a cosigner to get financing or a retired
individual with poor credit rating. It could be
someone who is just lonely needing only to talk
with somebody!

"Quickly learn to qualify and accurately
evaluate prospective buyers. Capture those who
have potential and release those who will simply
waste your time. After all you only get
commissions from real "now" buyers.

"But, let me stress, **NO** consumer should
be allowed to leave the car lot without several
salesmen having a chance at selling them.
Forget this fact and you may stand a good
chance at being fired by one of the roving
Generals.

"The first basics to selling is to capture
and qualify. Then apply further excite-to-buy
techniques only to these qualified buyers. Give
him a demonstration ride. Lead the consumer
into your sales office. Make whatever tentative
offer you must to make this happen!

"Once inside the sales office, the sales team
can *now* take control of the buyer and introduce
him to the real deal in the form of several shock
treatments. To be specific four shock treatments
are usually required. They are: the trade-in,
price of the car, down payment and the monthly
payment.

"Remember, impulse buying is the number
1 downfall for the consumer. The number 2
downfall is the monthly payment. A consumer

will forget all the other profit-taking areas of the deal just to get the right monthly payment.

"Now go out there and capture some prospects, qualify them and bring them to me. I'll explain the paper game we play in greater detail when you get another customer inside your sales office."

(Mr. Clark, our private, gets another prospective customer into his sales office. He starts to fill out some forms, but begins to lose the customer's interest. He quickly remembers one of his first lessons, team work, so he calls on Lieutenant Roberts for assistance. The lieutenant is at his post right outside the sales office ready to assist any of his frontline troopers!)

**Lieutenant Roberts:** (To customer) "Your trade-in car—ahh—tell me a little more about it!"

Leaving the sales office to report to his "General," he spots Mr. Clark guarding his post.

**Lieutenant Roberts:** "That was great thinking today when we almost lost that buyer. Your sitting in a chair in front of the exit saved the deal!

"Who knows, with a little more hard *work*, you could even become a lieutenant in a couple of years. But for *now* just get out there and get me more business capture more profits for our dealership! I'll take over and close this deal.

"By the way, the best salesman of the month earns a $200.00 reward. Could you use the money?"

As we leave our Private Clark in his first days at the dealership, we see him filled with pride and blind allegiance. Walking his post, anxiously awaiting his next encounter with a prospective buyer. Ever mindful that without sales (at any cost?) he'll be without **A JOB!**

## ADVANCED TRAINING

Let's take a more serious position in the art-of-selling. There is little written information on the verbal game of selling cars. Especially on the paper games car salesman persist in using on the general public.

The auto-industry has several training schools for car salesmen. I question their true ability to produce effective profit-takers for today's car dealerships. Car dealerships pride themselves on the number of "expert" sellers they possess. These "experts" are valuable because of the dollars taken during the dealing process. Rarely though are these "experts" in the majority at any particular dealership. Usually these "experts" represent the top third of the sales team and take in 80% of the car selling profits.

I will try to document this verbal selling game in writing. Shall we begin. Car dealers prefer youthful salesmen to greet their prospective buyers. They are less intimidating than the "expert" seller. These "greeters" play an important part for the sales team in setting up the buyer. In fact, the dealership consumes these youths at an alarming rate. I would guess five out of a hundred succeed in staying employed for more than a year. These "greeters" are a good "image" with the rest of the sales team working behind the scenes at the dealership.

Once the youth is hired, he is expected to perform immediately!That is, begin to capture and greet the prospective buyers with the zestful excitement of a novice. These novices will be sent out in the field—the car lot, for some "shock" treatment. The young salesman discovers quickly the difficulty in capturing the car buyer and taking control of the selling situation. The young salesman is quickly disciplined for letting the buyer escape the lot. The salesman's mentor will alert him of their errors, that all prospective buyers will be turned over to another salesman before letting them leave the car lot. Car salesmen who fail to obey this rule risk their employment at the car dealership. The youthful seller is rewarded for turning over the potential-buyer. If the buyer is sold, the first and last sellers will split the commission. The "greeter" will submit to the sales team's code of conduct or leave the dealership.

Once the beginning seller becomes a team player, setting up the buyer becomes a snap. Further requirements of the beginning seller will be demanded, though, before he may become a successful salesman."Walking" the buyers around the car lot and releasing them to another fellow car salesman is not enough to stay employed.

The next selling skill the beginning seller must master is qualifying the buyers prior to "walking" them into the selling-room. This is not difficult to learn for most consumers are willing to discuss their private affairs with others. The salesman easily takes advantage of this consumer "weakness." The salesman follows up with some friendly gestures and "private" conversations of his own. This selling strategy relaxes the buyer during the sale. This pseudo-friendship must last for several hours or until the sale is complete. To qualify the buyers, the salesman will need to know if they are employed, have a bank account, and do they rent or own their home. All very basic, but required business for the sales team to proceed with the sale.

Of course, the young car salesman doesn't realize his involvement in the selling game, until several months into the job. It's at this time he must decide to "marry" this selling situation or leave the job for another.

I have even discovered a car dealership that exploits high school students. These "special" sellers will experience success in the auto-industry as long as they continue *supplying* friends and relatives to the sales team.

Anyway, the beginning seller quickly discovers the cost of becoming a car salesman. He will get to "witness" fellow peers in motion. I did this willingly! And in a short time I was in the top third taking big profits for the sales team. Today, a top third-ranked seller makes around $80, 000. Keep in mind, this kind of money can only be made at aggressive car dealerships in your area.

The beginner-seller must release his prospective buyers to a fellow team player. To explain, each dealership has several sales teams complete with a closer working for them. Typically, a sales team consists of five salesmen (Frontliners) and one closer (the team's boss). To release a prospective buyer to another team's salesman, the beginning-salesman risks losing his job. Only the "expert" sellers may release a prospective buyer to another team's player. The dealership tolerates this infraction of the rules because the "expert" takes big dollars during the dealing process. At one dealership, I walked many a customer to these "expert's" private selling rooms. I shared in none of the commissions. These customers return to the same salesman year in and year out. Little did they know the financial risks to their wallet. They just liked the man, they would say. The entire auto industry loves this type of customer.

At each dealership, I would discover who these "experts" were. Then I would release a few prospective buyers to them to "witness" their selling strategies. Often these "experts" would sense my motives and not allow me to "witness" any more of their selling secrets. I suppose the only reason I was not fired from this particular dealership was because I too usually took big dollars from the customer. My closer would have to do very little in finalizing the sale. In other words, enough money was taken earlier in the deal, the only task the closer had to do was discount and close. This is the sign of a strong seller. Anyway, this "store" contained the most aggressive sales team I had ever worked for. So keep in mind not all dealerships are equal! Each dealership has a sales force. Some are weak and some are strong. Also, realize the dealership's sales *management* controls both their sales teams and customers during the selling process. Failure to comply with the management's wishes warrants disciplinary action.

Let's summarize the beginner salesman's responsibilities within the sales team.

Beginning salesmen learn by experience, not study.

Beginning salesmen are "shocked" into responsible team players.

Beginning salesmen must release their customers to "witness" the sell in motion.

Beginning salesmen must conform to the seller's code of conduct.

Beginning salesmen "marry" the sales teams' cause to take profit.

Beginning salesmen must please both their customer's and the management's ears.

Before the salesman's closer will consider working for the beginning salesman, several other requirements will be made of him. After capturing the prospective buyer, the salesman will "lead" or "walk" the customers around the car lot. During the "walking" phase of the sale, the salesman will qualify the customer. After the demonstration-ride, the salesman will "walk" them into the selling room.

The beginning salesman will continue to "control" the customer inside the selling room. Usually the credit application will be taken, a form of soft selling. The buyer responds easily here. The buyer begins to answer questions, a form of relaxation. The salesman continues relaxing the customer with small talk.

As more time is being invested inside the selling room, the salesman will start "shocking" the customers gently, as if by accident! At the end of the selling process, the customer will be "shocked" in a deliberate manner, and on purpose! After the credit application is near completion, the salesman will bring forward a WORKSHEET. This worksheet is designed to control both the sellers and the buyers and consists of four sections:

1) THE TRADE-IN;
2) THE PRICE OF NEW CAR;
3) THE DOWNPAYMENT; and
4) THE MONTHLY PAYMENTS.

Let's take a look at each section separately and see how car salesmen work their "magic" (See Figure 1 on next page).

Before we start, I wish to discuss the deliberate use of certain words in the salesman's vocabulary. Successful car salesmen discover quickly how to remain noncommittal in their conversation with the customer. The use of words like will, is, shall be, etc are avoided. In place of these words the salesman would use, maybe, I think, I will try, and possibly. This allows the seller to remain vague, and ambiguous with the customer. It is important

| TRADE-IN | PRICE OF NEW CAR |
|---|---|
| DOWNPAYMENT | MONTHLY PAYMENTS |

**Figure 1**

to avoid committing to any promises early in the sale. Leaving the selling process open for the closer to take additional profits is a skill required of all beginning car salesmen!

## THE TRADE-IN

The beginning-seller's task is to convince the buyers their trade-in lacks value with the dealership. Also, the buyers must *feel* they're going to win in the end. The seller must verbally stimulate the buyers into his selling room, to rally them into buying TODAY! To encourage the buyers, the seller may imply an inflated worth (imaginary) to the buyer's trade-in, called highballing the customer. Or the seller may give an ideal selling price on the new car being considered, called lowballing the customer. The salesman's strategy being to say anything and everything to get the buyer inside the SELLING ROOM!

If the salesman uses either or both of these verbal games, he must switch the buyers back to reality inside the selling. This "taking back" of verbal promises is a form of bait & switch—considered not honest when done on paper. If the closer is given the task of "taking back" the verbal promises made by the first salesman, usually less money is taken in the deal. It depends on how strong the closer is and how much effort he wants to apply to complete the sale. If too much work is required to "save" the deal, the closer may replace the beginning-seller with another.

The trade-in is the first area the seller deals with. The task being to capture the trade for much less than wholesale. For example, let's say the trade-in is worth about $4,000 and is considered in good running condition. The salesman must first begin with presenting an extra low figure to "shock" the buyers; he may then tell them that their car is just like a resent trade, taken in last week. That particular trade-in yielded only $1,500. After stating this bit of shocking news to the buyers, the seller will place a higher number on the worksheet, say $2,000 to make them "feel" good (See Figure 2).

After placing the $2,000 trade-in figure on the worksheet,

```
┌─────────────────────────────────────┐
│  TRADE-IN      │                     │
│                │                     │
│  2,000         │                     │
│    200         │                     │
│     100        │                     │
│      50        │                     │
│                │                     │
│ ───────────────┼──────────────────  │
│                │                     │
│                │                     │
│                │                     │
│                │                     │
│                │                     │
└─────────────────────────────────────┘
```

**Figure 2**

the salesman will await a reply from the buyer. The salesman may even encourage the buyers to defend their trade-in equity. Usually the buyer needs no encouragement and swiftly replies verbally! The salesman will listen for sometime, then increase the trade-in's worth a few hundred dollars. The buyers are stunned even amazed at how little they are rewarded for their verbal efforts in this matter. The salesman will remain calm and say, "Well, maybe in your case, the trade is worth much more." After listening to the buyers' demand for more trade-in money, the seller again increases the trade-in worth another few hundred dollars. This selling strategy *blows* the wind out of the buyers' "sails" and further "shocks" them into the fact their car is worth very little to the dealership. Usually the salesman will switch back to the credit application to reduce the buyer's sharpness towards the sale, in general. If the buyer is resistant, the seller will back off entirely, turning over the customer to another salesman, or simply talk about something else like vacations, fishing, sports, etc.

After a short while, the salesman will return to the worksheet, and reward the buyer with another even smaller trade-in dollar increase. In any event, the salesman is ready to *cross over* to the next section on the worksheet, THE PRICE OF THE NEW CAR. To smooth over the transition, the salesman may indicate that he's not the appraiser and wishes the buyer the greatest of success in capturing the highest trade-in dollars available.

## THE PRICE OF THE NEW CAR

The beginning seller's task is to continue the hope of the buyer at WINNING during the sale and to continue stimulating them "verbally" about their new car purchase. "Expert" sellers always assume their customer will buy TODAY. Their entire conversation presents the buyer as already *proud new car owners.*

As you can see, the worksheet is controlling both the seller and the buyers. That each section has a purpose, a goal, for its user the upper management. The beginning salesman continues his control of the selling situation by placing the full selling price of the new car on the worksheet. The seller awaits the buyer's reply. If none, the seller will encourage some sort of conversation with the buyers. This allows the salesman time to resolve any objections the buyers may have about the sale to this point. If a low-ball figure was given, out on the car lot, the salesman may simply reply, "the boss requires the full selling price be placed on the worksheet for his reference." The seller's mission being to not discount the price of the new car too early in the deal (See Figure 3).

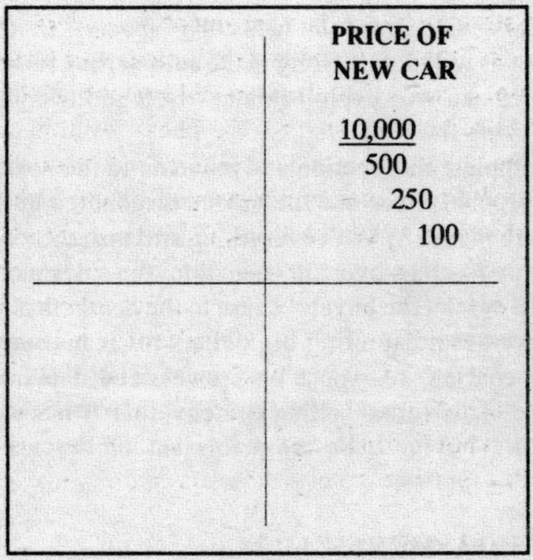

PRICE OF
NEW CAR

<u>10,000</u>
500
250
100

Figure 3

After placing the full selling price on the worksheet, the salesman will begin the second "shock" treatment. The salesman will underline the full price of the car and offer a $500 discount, stating he is authorized to discount this car for a *today sale*. The salesman then awaits the buyers' reply. Usually, the buyers will chat for some time. In fact, the salesman will encourage them to continue this chat even in their defense. After a short while, the salesman will interrupt the conversation (taking control) and place another discount figure on the price of the new car (See

Figure 3). The salesman will again await the buyers' reply, even encourage them to discuss the offer in detail. If the buyers continue to demand more discounted dollars off the new car, the seller will CROSS-OVER to the trade-in section, or for a "softer" selling area return to the credit application to confound and confuse the buyers. After the buyers cool down, the seller will return to the PRICE OF THE NEW CAR section.

Often the seller will act sensitive to the buyers' position and call on them to become friends again. That he is really on their side and that most customers who buy from him are WINNERS! The beginning salesman who lacks this "special" trait to become instant friends will not last long in the auto-selling industry! Later on, the salesman will exploit this newly found friendship in the name of saving the deal.

To complete this section and move on to the next, the salesman will probably increase the buyers discounted dollars on the new car (see Figure 3).With everything still unresolved, the salesman is ready to cross over. In transition, the salesman may indicate he will defend the buyers' cause to the *death*, that he "works" for the buyer, that capturing big dollars off is his specialty. The seller may continue to expose his prowess and state my "friends" always win! This verbal selling strategy, that "I'm on your side," prepares the buyer to be most tolerant of the seller's game playing.

## THE DOWNPAYMENT

It is here that reality finally sets in and "shocks" the buyers. Many car salesmen know at this time in the sale the buyer may *bolt* from the selling room. Especially when the buyers realize the financial liabilities on ones bank account and pay check. It is here, the seller must reconfirm his friendship to the buyers. It is now that the beginning seller will become firm, even demanding. The seller will request some cash from the buyers. He will demand some visibility to the buyers' *today cash* on the negotiating table!

The seller will do most of the talking in this section. He may "cross over" to another worksheet section if the buyers get too nervous or upset. Again, the safest paperwork section being the credit application. Even so, several downpayment figures (requests) will be placed on the worksheet to swiftly "shock" the buyers into the reality of the sale (see Figure 4). The salesman will remind the buyers that they are required to hand over some cash in exchange for the new car. The salesman will remind the buyers that they are taking delivery of the new car *today*! In any event the salesman is preparing to "cross over" to the final section on the worksheet, THE MONTHLY PAYMENTS. To smooth over the transition, from DOWNPAYMENT to MONTHLY PAYMENTS, the salesman may indicate he's not required to take possession of any downpayment monies yet, but only need some "good faith" dollars to show management you're real *today buyers!*

## THE MONTHLY PAYMENTS

The beginning seller's task is to continue the buyers hope of WINNING during the sale. The seller must continue stimulating

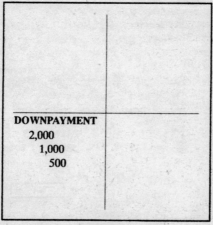

**DOWNPAYMENT**
2,000
1,000
500

**Figure 4**

the buyers' ears "verbally" about their excellent choice of car. The seller will continue to rally the buyers into a *today purchase*! The beginner seller's secondary task is to establish a monthly range for the closer and the buyers. The closer's task is to take that information before the buyers and imply great savings are at hand. In reality, the buyers will be "tricked" into thinking they won at the car buying process.

To enter this worksheet section properly, the seller must set up the buyer with caution! It is here too, the buyers may *bolt* from the selling room.And it is here, the buyers may terminate the "friendship" the seller worked so hard to develop. The beginning seller will "verbally" bring forward an extremely high monthly payments figure for the buyers to "witness" on the worksheet. In fact, this figure will be joined by another still ambiguous monthly figure (See Figure 5). Except the second figure will be much lower than the first. Of course, the buyers "feel" they got a discount, somewhere on the worksheet, but they are not sure where! This selling ploy will be played over and over until the buyers

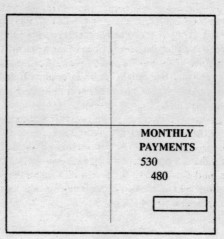

**Figure 5**

aren't sure they're winning or losing. This is the most *valuable* skill the seller can have. Usually the buyer's only concerns are how much are my monthly payments and what am I getting for my trade. This consumer weakness costs the general public *billions of dollars every year*! If you wish to be a car salesman, you must master this verbal skill. You really have no choice in the matter, the sales team will override your intentions, anyway for the sake of taking profit.

The first figure written on the worksheet's monthly payments section will be extremely high. For example, let's say $530 (See Figure 5). This figure may be several hundreds of dollars higher than a "fair" deal. The beginning-seller will await the buyers' reply. Sort of letting the monthly payments figure sink in to the buyers' minds. Next, the seller may chat about a possible discounted dollars figure in the form of lower monthly payments! Then the seller will "act" on the side of the buyers and place a much lower monthly payments figure on the worksheet. Again, the seller awaits the buyers' reply. This time he will encourage the buyers to speak up, even rejoice, over the lower monthly payments offered. By "shocking" the buyers with both a high and then lower monthly payment, the seller reconfirms his "friendship." Of course, nothing is final until approved by the management! Also, by reducing the monthly payments, the seller doesn't need to adjust the selling price of the new car. This is important, because if the buyers asked for clarification on this matter, the seller would be "caught" in his sales ploy. If this happens, usually the seller will *turn over the buyers to another team player, maybe even his closer, to save the deal.*

After several reductions in the monthly payments and a lot of chatting from the seller, the buyers are ready for TURNING OVER to the closer. The seller will summarize the buyers' offer (really it's the seller's offer in disguise) and remind the buyers that he is on their side! The seller will pick up all the paperwork and leave the selling room not forgetting to take any "holding money" captured earlier from the buyers.

*Does the reader sense the degree of difficulty the beginning-seller has at keeping his job at a local dealership—that capturing and "walking" the buyer is not enough to stay employed! I think the dealership's sales team just asks too much of its young sellers; To expect them to "shock" the buyers with a plan of assisting the closer, to "verbally" bait & switch the buyers on a worksheet. To not commit "verbally," or in writing, to remain vague, even general, so the rest of the sales team can take additional profits is very forward of the dealership's management. I suppose that's why few young sellers stay employed for more than six months at aggressive "dealerships in America.*

## THE CLOSER'S CLASSIC ACT

The closer, the salesman's boss, must take over in a "I'm in control" manner. He will be strong in voice, even firm, but friendly with the buyers. The closer's task is to continue the hope of the buyer at WINNING during the sale. He will continue the beginning-seller's efforts to stimulate the buyers "verbally" about the new car purchase. The closer always assumes the buyers are *today buyers*! The closer's secondary task is to search the worksheet for additional opportunities to take cash! If this closer fails to take maximum dollars from the buyers, the management will send in another closer to complete this "classic act"!

The closer will slowly, but surely, take away any and all offers the first salesman gave to the buyers. He will accomplish this task by CROSSING OUT the dollar figures in the various worksheet sections. In other words, the closer is both taking away and adding worksheet-dollars to assure maximum profit for the dealership (See Figure 6 on next page).

The closer will continue to "shock" the buyers in what it takes to purchase a new car. Each time, the closer will await the buyers' reply. This process will continue until the trade-in's appraisal figure is brought inside the selling room. The appraisal

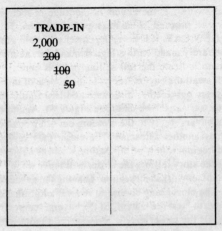

**Figure 6**

figure will not be far off from the first salesman's estimates. In fact, few consumers realize a major goal of the sales the sales team is to capture your trade-in way below its true worth, if possible, in thousand dollar bills! Later, these same sellers will resell your trade-in for several thousands over wholesale. In many a deal, more dollars are taken from the trade-in then from the new car purchase.This suggests, the best sellers hold out in the used car department. You would be correct in believing that! Most "expert" sellers are based in this highly profitable selling area—the used car lot. If a new car salesman crosses into the used car lot with a customer, he will have to release them to the used car "experts." A sort of a penalty on the younger sellers for not selling their customer a new car. On the other hand, if a used car salesman captures a buyer, who persists in buying a new car, he may freely walk the customer over to the new car department and proceed to sell them for maximum profits. Most car dealerships pride themselves on the number of the "aggressive" sellers because they too enjoy in taking their share of the profits of a sale. Ethics is not debated inside the selling room!

After "working" the buyers in the trade-in section, usually the closer will proceed to the next worksheet area, THE PRICE OF THE NEW CAR. It is here, the closer will hold ground. Discounts are rarely made on this high demand car, he may say any comments to indicate the full selling price is here to stay! The closer will await the buyers' reply. In the middle of this reply, the closer *crosses out* another discounted dollars figure and maybe another, to *feel out* the buyers (See Figure 7). Again, the closer awaits the buyers' reply to the crossing out of discounted dollars *promised* by another salesman. The closer may reply, the first seller is a beginner, new at the business, and is subject to error. Whatever the story telling, the closer will move on, by "crossing over" to another worksheet section. Leaving the new car price unresolved. The closer may choose to request additional downpayment dollars to "test the waters" of the buyers' temperament (See Figure 7). Or the closer may *give-in* and add more trade-in dollars (See Figure 8 on next page), or begin "working" a new

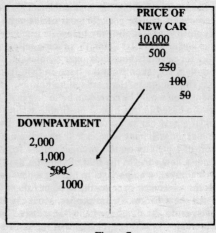

**Figure 7**

172

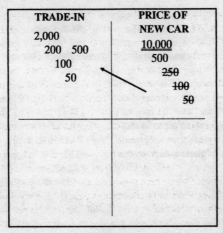

**Figure 8**

worksheet section, THE MONTHLY PAYMENTS SECTION. Whatever the closer decides, it will be for the purpose to take more profits from the buyers. The closer is very special to the sales team. They are "experts" at their trade! They can "dance"on the worksheet with great skill. I must take my hat off to them and salute their gamesmanship in the art of control.The straight sell houses are loaded with these masters of the tongue and pen!

The closer will finally cross over into the most important worksheet section, THE MONTHLY PAYMENTS (see Figure 9 on next page). The closer knows when the buyers have been "shocked" enough. The closer will perform his "magic" in the final act of taking a profit. It's ironic, in this section, the buyers are made to feel they have won!

The closer will reduce the monthly payments to make the buyers feel that he (the closer) is worried about the deal. This reduction in monthly payments is often sizable (See Figure 9). In exchange for this "favor," the closer will demand additional downpayment dollars, or cross over into the trade-in section and

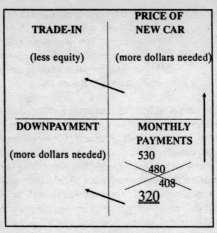

**Figure 9**

*cross out* additional trade-in dollars. The buyers rarely realize the earlier salesman's involvement in setting them up for the closer. Usually, the buyers still consider the first salesman a "good" guy, a "friend" in need! Isn't that amazing.

Each time the closer reduces the monthly payments, he will *cross over* to another section and take more worksheet profits.

The buyer, on the other hand, senses victory! They are getting lower payments! In fact, the buyers often *forgive* the closer for his rudeness in their dealings with him. When the closer has more then enough profit to close the deal, he will report to the management for further instructions, but not before repeating the agreed upon figures concluded on the worksheet. Usually, only three figures are repeated: the trade-in's selling price to the dealer; the downpayment needed to take delivery of the new car *today*, and the monthly payments.

Author's question:  *What vital figure is missing from the above data? Why aren't the buyers concerned with that figure? Is not this figure vital to the buyers pocketbook?*

*If you can answer this question, concentrate on why the seller avoided releasing that information. You will have stumbled on the central core to the closer's game plan: to leave room for others to take additional profit if management deems fit!*

After returning from the manager's office, the closer carries out his instructions. What transpires depends on the "aggressiveness" of the sales team's management. The closer may be directed to take additional add-on dollars—adding dealer options to the new car—or simply close the deal. The worst thing that could happen is another closer be introduced to *take over* both the buyers and the deal. This would mean, the buyers will be "worked" for additional dollars in a big way! This *recycling the buyers* has a purpose. Maybe the buyers revealed a rather large bank account figure on their credit application. Management may wish to capture a portion of that "easy" cash as part of the deal.

Usually, the closer will return to the selling room demanding additional cash to save the deal (for the buyers' sake). The closer may indicate management has discovered an error on the paperwork. Whatever the sales ploy, it will be made to continue the sale for additional cash. If the buyers relent to this request for more cash, the closer will "hide" this cash somewhere on the contract. Remember, the dealership takes its money off the top! In other words, any up front cash, the buyers delivered to the closer, is subject to be *hidden*; by placing it in non-equity areas on the contract. The bank only recognizes the true worth of the car. The bank will accept the financing paper from the dealer, if certain requirements are met. The "paper" will be bought, by the bank, for the wholesale value of the new car plus tax and license. Any monies captured above that figure may become the property of the dealership their profit!

If the closer returns to close the sale, usually the younger salesman will be present to "witness" the signing of the contract. The closer will swiftly discuss the contract details asking the buyers to initial several key areas. Often the younger salesman becomes chatty, during the signing. This usually distracts the buyers enough to keep them off-balance, during the review of the contract.

After the signing of the contract, the closer will collect all downpayment money due, and the title and licensing documents will be signed. Usually, the buyer fails to notice any details on the contract. Often, they can't even remember the final *selling price of the new car, or even the length of the contract that will bind them for many years. It's all too exciting to be driving in another of "Detroit's best efforts" to be concerned with such minor details as debt.*

Author's comment: *I hope the above effort will assist you in your dealings with the sellers at your local dealership. Friendly or not, the sales team and its management have only one goal—to take profit. In most of my 2,000 radio and television interviews, car salesmen commonly rebuttal my comments, they resent the words "taking profit." But this is exactly what happens inside thousands of car dealerships across our great land. I believe, the automobile manufacturers of cars would "shake-in-their-boots" if they were delegated the task of selling to the general public. It's sad! These manufacturer's cannot control the sellers of their products!*

*As far as the difficulty of selling the buyer, first verbally, secondly on the worksheet, and lastly on contract must be quite a dramatic shock for the beginning-salesman. To succeed in this profession, the beginning-salesman must survive both his peers and the dealership's management. Even so, if you are seriously considering becoming a seller of a product or service, consider becoming a car salesman for a short while. You will never forget the experience! Any short period of experience in this selling profession will reward you in big dollars, usually later in another selling occupation!*

One other comment!

*"Aggressive" sales teams working at car dealerships, verbally take profits. The better players take even more profits from today's consumers. I believe for every sales dollar captured by these "aggressive" sellers, 50 cents is unnecessarily lost by the customer. In other words, the sellers enjoy excess profits due to their verbal bait & switch games played on the public inside the "private" selling room.*

# CHAPTER TWELVE

# THE RADIO INTERVIEW

"Hey, there. This is Tony Talken...it's 2:00 and time for the K.A.R.S. Consumer Corner! Today we have with us, Mr. Darrell Parrish, a former car salesman and author of *THE CAR BUYERS ART—How to Beat the Salesman at his Own Game*.

"Now we've all had our own experiences at buying a car, so let's listen to a teacher in the art of car-buying.

"Remember, the number to call is 858-5525 or, outside the 269 area code, the number is 746-2727! So let's hear from you, because you're why we're here.

"But first a word from the people who pay the bills, our sponsor.

"OK we're back now!

So you think you're ready to buy a car. You heard about the sting, the scam, and the flim-flam, now let us fill you in on the verbal scam. By skimming a bit here and a bit there, the "professional" salesman and his sales team takes the average buyer for a ride in more ways than one. Like a lamb to the slaughter, the car salesman will lead you through a sequence of selling events designed to relieve you of big dollars, in exchange for an automobile, maybe one you aren't even sure you want.

We're talking with Darrell Parrish, author of *THE CAR BUYERS ART*.

TONY: Darrell, it appears to me that on the surface your book is a how to get even type of literature, but is it really?

DARRELL: I think originally the book was slanted that way. I chose to test this book's concepts and ideas within a college. California State University at Long Beach was kind enough to provide me with both a classroom and students. This teaching effort lasted about four years. The students provided an invaluable service. They thinned out THE *CAR BUYERS ARTS*' useless information. It's now packed with enough "working" information to make the car buying effort both enjoyable and profitable for any one concerned with buying a car.

The book provides the reader the complete selling gameplan car salesmen persist playing on the general public. That is, it provides the master plan sellers use to confuse and confound the buyer during the selling process.

Let me state that this book is not saying, "Let's go out and cheat the car dealership out of a profit." It is a book that provides the consumer with a complete set of buying plans for an easy victory with today's aggressive car salesmen. I do suggest readers of this book to digest its information slowly! This book doesn't promote any cheating or lying on the part of the consumer. If the sales team persists in such habits, you should leave the dealership for another.

TONY: Why is car buying so difficult, and for many of us, so painful?

DARRELL: I believe the dealerships makes this happen on

purpose. In the past, car buying was simple—cash for car! In those days, financing a car was not as common as today; everyone was a cash buyer and few selling games could be played on the buyer. Today, unfortunately, car dealers discovered, complexing the buying process, both verbally and on paperwork, could yield additional profits.

After World War II, these aggressive car dealerships focused their selling games and strategies in an arena where most profits could be taken—inside the selling room! Little did the public know to what extent the car dealer would go! Today, few consumers survive the car salesman encounter. They stumble and fall inside the car dealership's selling rooms, economically speaking!

TONY: Outside of a house, the biggest item a person or family can purchase is a car.

DARRELL: Tony, I really wonder about that statement. Are houses more expensive than cars? Generally, families purchase less houses than cars. In fact, a typical family may purchase over 10-15 cars in their lifetime. If you focus on cars, as consumable goods and not equity like real estate, you soon realize the economical losses cars bring on families.

TONY: What are some of the unnecessary risks that a car buyer may eliminate?

DARRELL: First is depreciation. Cars are splitting into two major camps, the "throw-aways" and the so called "luxury" models. Both depreciate for different end-of-the-road reasons. The "throw-away" models lose additional resale value because the public perceives them useless after a certain odometer reading, not worthy of a second owner! Therefore, when it comes time to sell or trade, few potential buyers will consider your offer seriously. Of course, the dealer will, and at a substantial loss to you.

The "luxury" models suffer additional resale value too! Even though these models depreciate heavily as all other cars do, few customers will come forward with cash because of the high cost as a used car. The consumer would rather purchase a new, less expensive model from a dealership. Of course, the dealer will help you out at trade-in time with a sizable equity loss, providing you buy one of their's. The loss can be in the thousands of dollars below wholesale.

I suggest you consider only cars that are easy to resell—the high demand cars! Some of them depreciate very little during their use and are easy to resell when you're done with them. The automobile manufacturers will not tell you which ones they are. So, you need to do some homework. Just price out the new car of choice. Then instantly age it (new car) two years! If the wholesale value of this"aged"car is less than 50% of the asking price, I suggest you choose another model or make of car.

TONY:    I see, we don't want to just buy any car on the lot. We want to purchase high valued cars, the ones that depreciate the least in the marketplace as used cars. I think I bought the wrong car, Darrell!

DARRELL:    Tony, the next time you're in the marketplace for

TONY: You mentioned off the air about a "blue book." Where are these books found?

DARRELL: The Kelly Blue Book is a reference book on retail and wholesale values on used cars. The industry follows this book faithfully. They are found at most banks, libraries and credit unions.

TONY: What other risks can be eliminated for today's car buyers?

DARRELL: Eliminate the desire to impulse buy. You need to prepare yourself before approaching the car dealership. Car buying is exciting. It's easy to make mistakes. The salesman seizes any opportunity to confuse and confound the buyer. Also, I suggest shopping and buying on separate days.

TONY: Darrell, how can we get a large discount off the selling price of a used car?

DARRELL: Remember, the selling price on the window is only the asking price. The final selling price depends on your negotiating skills and patience. By limiting the available downpayment and cash in the total offer, you may capture a below wholesale price, on any used car, if you dare to ask!

TONY: Yes, and talking about asking, most salesmen seem to just go on and on asking all sorts of questions! How does a person guard himself against giving out too much information?

185

DARRELL: Well, you have to recognize that not every question deserves an answer. The salesman does have a basic responsibility to qualify you as a "real buyer." So questions, such as "Are you employed, do you have a down payment, do you have a savings and checking account, are to be expected. But other questions or statements may be designed to lead or excite you into buying a car now today.

TONY: OK, thank you. Now we have to break again but when we come back we'll take our first caller. The number again is 858-5525 and outside area code 269 the number is 746-2727.

JINGLE

TONY: We're here today with Darrell Parrish and we're talking about how to beat the car salesman at his own game. Here's our first call. Go ahead, you're on the air.

CALLER #1: Why do you people always make these salesmen out to be some kind of highway robber. Both my husband and my son sell cars and I assure you that they not only have to work very hard for their money but they do it honestly! And I love them both dearly. I think you're the one that's trying to rip off the public with your book!!

DARRELL: I agree that mothers should love their sons. They can be very protective, at times. I would hope that my mother continued loving me during my time as a car salesman. As for your husband, I suggest you "witness" some of his selling tactics inside the selling-room. If that doesn't bother you and your image of him, then continue to support his quest to make a living. Most auto indus-

186

try critics fail to read *THE CAR BUYER'S ART* and instead lash out at my efforts to teach, as if I'm a villain. Maybe it's their subconscious feelings that bother them.

TONY: I think mothers would love their sons no matter what their occupations. OK, here's our next caller.

CALLER#2: Yeah, ahh, I'd like to ask Mr. Parrish if someone I know refers me to a particular dealer or salesman, should I feel that they're going to give me a fair deal?

DARRELL: You're asking if referrals are valuable? In most cases, yes. The exception is the sales department at car dealers. After all, no salesman is going to be able to keep his job for long if he doesn't work toward getting the maximum profit for the dealer. You must have excellent negotiating skills to effectively compete with car salesmen. Referrals get you to a specific dealership and salesman. How successful you become inside the salesman's office depends on your ability to compete with them. And with a sales team backing up the salesman, you need every negotiating skill available!

CALLER#2: In other words, you are on your own inside the salesman's office. The salesman's on his own side! Always! OK, well, one other question. Will buying a car with cash give me any more bargaining power?

TONY: Very good point. Won't the sight of all that green stuff excite the salesman into giving you what you want?

DARRELL: In most cases no! Because the banks issue a paid-

187

in-full check in exchange for your contract from the dealer. That's just good business for both the bank and car dealership. I suggest you approach the dealership's sales team as a monthly payment buyer. Then near the end of the deal, convert back to your original plan of being a cash buyer. With the time invested in you and your exposed American dollars, how can the dealer resist in not giving you the "best deal in town"—yours.

TONY:      So, what you're saying is dealers consider everyone a cash buyer. And when walking into the dealer, playing monthly payments-buyer works for you.

DARRELL:   That's right. Even though you'll still be making monthly payments to your own bank, as far as the dealer is concerned, you're a cash buyer.

TONY:      There always seems to be a lot of talk about import cars coming into the U.S. Will the Japanese increase the shipment of cars to America?

DARRELL:   Personally, I don't believe the Japanese imports will increase in any great quantity for the next few years. Possibly a yearly increase of cars will take place. The reason, I feel, will be that the Japanese product image will lose it's mystique in the American marketplace as the years go on. The Japanese are very patient and will slowly overtake the marketplace if you let them. A sort of warfare is being played—out here in our Homeland. If you let them.

For example: the import truck market is now saturated. No one is on a waiting list. Additional Dealership Markup Stickers are not seen and free media publicity is down to a nil. This will happen to other import cars, if the market becomes saturated with any particular make or model of car. The Japanese or any other import will not increase their shipments dramatically, if they stand to loose top dollars, or their market position in this country.

TONY: Are all dealerships the same? Do they all follow a set formula? A plan of action?

DARRELL: Well, there are at least two types of selling-games dealerships persist in using: the straight-sell house and turn-over house. The former is the oldest and most traditional. They are considered the softer, more gentler of the two profit-taking systems in the country. They're easy to spot— you will be dealing with one salesperson during the selling process. Somehow, the public perceives these sales teams as the lesser of two evils.

The other selling system is the newest and most notorious. Their sales teams are aggressive and great role players. They take big dollars from today's car buyers. You will quickly realize you're in their grasp, when you see several sales people working the deal.

TONY: Is the car buyer supposed to choose their dealership?

DARRELL: I suggest the car buyer be able to distinguish between the two. Both types of selling houses take big profits when the customer lets them. On the other hand, the prepared buyer has little problem with either of these selling houses. To them they are both fun to deal with. I enjoy the turn-over

189

houses and practice with them for the fun of it! Then, when I'm serious about buying a car, I work over several of these dealers, slowly! To warm up! (If you practice on several of these dealers, you will soon realize car salesmen talk alike.) I then enter a straight-sell house for the real purchase. If I don't fair well in the deal, I escape for another and another, until I win! If I must, I will even consider, competing with the sellers in a turn-over house for maximum savings! It's just more work for me.

Dealership sales teams are practicing with another form of selling-game. They employ women to encounter potential buyers. These saleswomen are called, "greeters." Their primary task is to capture the customer on the car lot. Then say everything and anything to get the customer inside the selling room. Once inside the selling room, "real" car salesmen will enter and take over. To me, this is a form of bait & switch. That is, the sales team baits you with a less intimidating seller (a greeter), and turns you over to a more professional seller—THE ACTUAL CAR SALESMAN! The greeters are paid a fee for walking the customer into the selling room. I have had many salesmen (not car salesmen), tell me they resent this practice deeply!

TONY:          Why has the marketplace let this happen?

DARRELL:     The DMV are the policemen to the industry. They issue selling licenses to car salesmen, including their managers. Few people realize that without these permits, car salesmen could not sell cars. I have suggested, for years, that if you have a legal dispute with any salesman, take your complaint to a small claims court. Prove your claim before the court, and then proceed to the DMV for removal of the car salesman's license! Maybe then the car salesman and their selling partners will be more careful with what they say and do to the general public.

TONY:      If this selling process is illegal, why can't something be done?

DARRELL:   Tony, please remember, most of what has been said is verbal! If the selling game was in writing, on contract, lawyers could then document the game. Then the dealership could be in trouble. But it is not in writing. It's difficult to document a verbal bait and switch, because the only witnesses are the buyers and sellers—the buyers are not sure what is happening and the sellers will not disclose their strategies to the courts or the DMV.

TONY:      Can the dealership's sales team make a mistake and document their mischief, by accident?

DARRELL:   An excellent question! Yes, they are making mistakes on paper. The Manufacturer's Sticker at some dealers is being taken off and the figures altered. In other words, when you add up the options with the base price on the Manufacturer's Sticker, the numbers may be different between dealerships. I have even seen errors in addition on Dealer Markup Stickers that dealers attach to new cars.

Another area where car salesmen typically and willfully produce additional profits is during the "working up" of the deal on paper. Here, the car salesman intentionally makes errors to see if the buyers are watching.

| | |
|---|---|
| TONY: | Should not the marketplace reward the better player, be it seller or buyer? |
| DARRELL: | Yes! Providing both sides know the rules and play the game fairly. I think the better player should win! If the car buyer takes car buying seriously and plans for his car salesman encounter, the buying process is indeed a profitable experience for both. |
| TONY: | Darrell, you sound like a fair guy! What does the auto industry think of you? |
| DARRELL: | Most car salesmen are quiet; only the aggressive sellers are nervous when the media exposes their trade secrets. The most common rebuttal to my consumer education effort is that none of this exists. That everything is fictitious, a lie; that I must have been a weak seller to betray the industry. It would be fair to say, I dislike the turn-over houses and their persist selling games played on the general public. |
| TONY: | Darrell, just how do you purchase your cars? |
| DARRELL: | I use two approaches: I try to become an Ad-Car-Buyer. I let the salesman complex the ad car (usually only one on the lot) I'm interested in, for the sake of consuming time. Then I take control of both the salesman and the deal. Next, I revert back to the simple sale of the ad car (which yields little profit for both salesman and dealership). |
| | My other approach is to take the above buying strategy one step further. First, I locate an Ad car of interest, then complex the deal with additional options of interest (always factory installed equipment). Usually, the car with additional |

192

options is on the same car lot as the Ad car. As time is consumed, the dealer begins to realize, if things don't go my way, they will lose the sale. Finally they decide to sell the non-ad car to me at a substantial discount.

TONY: Will the auto industry change its selling habits?

DARRELL: Not willingly. I believe that one day the car buyer will make his car purchase from a bank, credit union or even a department store display. Also I believe the future car salesman will be restricted to selling only used cars, that the verbal bait and switch schemes will eventually become illegal selling practices. I think the consumer should have a fair chance at getting that right car at the right price. It's sad that there seems to be so many individuals in the auto industry dead set against this worthy consumer goal!

TONY: If the deal is thin and yields little profit to the dealership, what tactics would you expect from the sales team?

DARRELL: Well, you can expect one of two tactics. First, they will try several attempts to take profit right up to the signing of the contract.Or, they may even try removing some of the factory installed or dealer add-on options, if any, on the car you are about to purchase.

TONY: Why are there so many buyer services in the country?

DARRELL: I believe these services are here to fill a need and I question their effectiveness in helping the consumer save money. Remember, these brokers are really car sellers. Their desire to take profits are the same as car dealerships. I think their mere existence lends visibility to the injustice car dealerships successfully play on the general public.

TONY: Is there a selected group of people or occupation that car salesmen dislike?

DARRELL: Yes! It is the teaching profession. Teachers are hard to sell in the car salesmen's eyes. Not worth the effort! The teachers evidently "see" the verbal games played on them. Car salesmen don't like that. After reading and practicing this book's concepts and ideas, my students see the sellers game plan, too!

TONY: Just how does a car buyer communicate with the sellers?

DARRELL: Knowledge is necessary, of course, but it isn't enough. You also must do something with the facts. You must know *how*. And that means developing certain skills—primarily communication skills, both verbal and non-verbal. You have a much better chance of getting the car you want at the price you want, if you know how to communicate effectively. Knowing what to do and how to do it means that you don't subscribe to group thinking, talking, and doing. And it means that the salesman will have to work harder to sell you exactly what you want. Communicating is much more than knowing how to express yourself verbally. It's knowing when to talk and when to listen, how to be specific and not general and how to observe so that you can read and understand printed, verbal, and other non-verbal signs. It's all knowing when to ask questions and when to leave. Basically, it's knowing what to look for in the car lot, how to read the language of basic selling tactics and how to negotiate that fair deal for yourself or family. Knowing how to communicate gives you a large measure of control over the situation when car buying. You are less likely to be trapped, manipulated or switched to something you don't want. Let's face it, car buying is made difficult by dealers to maximize their profits. Being difficult to figure out, allows you an excellent chance at reducing the dealers take!

TONY:      Well, I think we only have time for a couple more calls...but first a word from our sponsor.

Alright, here we are again. We're talking with Darrell Parrish and about his book, *THE CAR BUYERS ART*—How to beat the salesman at his own game. Here's our next caller...go ahead you're on the air.

CALLER#3:      Hi, Tony, my name is Gloria...and I would like to ask Mr. Parrish if there are any reliable sources that will truthfully give me the facts on which cars to consider?

DARRELL:      Yes, I consider three publications to be very good sources. *Changing Times, Motor Trend* and *Consumer Reports*. These give an unbiased report on how well different cars perform and the quality of construction. After that, the only other factor is what car meets your needs and wants.

CALLER#4:      Yeah, good afternoon Tony, I'd like to ask your guest if car salesmen still try to switch you from a car you think you'd like to look at to another car that he wants you to look at?

| | |
|---|---|
| DARRELL: | Unfortunately, yes. Often there is, especially in used car lots, a car or cars the dealer's management would like to get rid of. The dealer may instruct or even apply pressure to their salesmen to sell those particular cars. If the salesmen don't make a real effort to sell them, they'll soon be looking for another job. |
| CALLER#5: | I'm a car salesman and I'm proud of it! I disagree with everything you have said. |
| TONY: | Would you be specific, sir! |
| CALLER#5: | This guy is a liar, a fake. He was probably a weak salesman at that. What's his beef against the auto industry, anyway? |
| TONY: | You are not asking a specific question. Please do, before I go to the next caller. |
| CALLER#5: | This guy is a !@#$....%^&*, !@#$.... |
| TONY: | Mr. Parrish, I guess you are used to upsetting car salesmen. |
| DARRELL: | Unethical salesmen get very upset with this type of consumer interest interview. They follow the contents of this radio interview easily because they are in the car selling business. Where as, the consumer may be just discovering the basics in car buying. These same unethical car salesmen enjoy long term employment living off referrals from past customers. I don't recommend the referral system for my readers as a general rule. If you are a prepared buyer and your friend is not, your friend will not fair well inside the selling room. You risk losing a friend for life. |

CALLER#6: What cautions can you offer about selling the trade-in to another private party?

DARRELL: Over half the country's population sells their cars to other private parties. When placing your ad in local newspapers you may be taking some unnecessary risks. Criminal elements in your area can easily target their victims (based on make of car offered for sale). It is suggested when selling your car, you locate the vehicle on a nearby business corner-lot (gas station, etc) with permission of property owner. When the prospective buyer call to meet you, make arrangements to meet at the car's location (daytime and with lots of people around). Further, it's suggested you let the prospective buyer test drive the car alone and for a short period of time—indicate others will be arriving soon to test drive the car. If the individual is of the criminal-type, you may lose your car, but be spared personal robbery or harm. It's best you bring friends along and collect your money before you sign over the title of ownership. Call your local Department of Motor Vehicles for further details and cautions.

TONY: How do you know your fair deal is for "real" or not?

DARRELL: The customer will have to be on his toes. The last few minutes of the selling process are where the final figures are hammered out. Usually at this time, the salesman's closer will leave and return to the selling room several times. Each time demanding additional dollars! If you are too high and your payments yield the necessary profits the dealer expects, then the deal will close quickly and painlessly! If the profits are thin for the seller, the same events should occur, except the sellers will be more aggressive, even rude, during the close of the sale. Usually it is a good sign the buyers are getting an excellent deal. So bare with the emotions these sellers play on you, some of them are for real!

TONY: What attitude should one take in competing for that fair deal?

DARRELL: As effective as knowledge and skills are, they can be easily sabotaged by attitude—specifically, the wrong attitude. The salesman is trained to read signs of weakness. He can smell fear, vagueness, shyness and indecisiveness a mile away. And he will make capitol of them.

Are you usually impatient, impulsive, talkative, defensive, vague, anxious or nervous? If so, the salesman will "love" you because he knows fear is lurking somewhere. And he will immediately cast you as a loser in a script that will have a happy ending for him. With a losing attitude, you most likely will buy in haste, repent in leisure. It's called "buyer's remorse."

To a large extent, no matter how knowledgeable and articulate you may be, your emotions will govern things. So...get rid of impatience, impulsiveness, your shyness and so on, or at least bring them under control. Otherwise, you may have to pay a high price for them at your local dealership. And the last thing you want to hear from your family and friends is, "I told you so!"

TONY: Are you suggesting to use the same aggressiveness as car salesmen use on the public?

DARRELL: Once you are in-the-know and prepared to compete with these sellers, I suggest you be friendly and humane. But don't strive to be popular! You're not in a popularity contest. Whether or not the salesman likes you has little or nothing to do with why you're there. You're not there to win his approval. You're there to make a fair exchange—your money for his car. So forget popularity. I get many phone calls from doctors and dentists when on radio talk shows. They typically tell me their best friends are car salesmen and that they buy all their cars from them. When they realize that excess money was taken from them in the name of friendship, they end the conversation in shock! I hope these dealers know what they're doing, because I suspect these "deceived" doctors and dentists may call-in their car selling friends for some exploratory surgery (and I don't know what doctors and dentists consider excess organs in the body!). Joking aside, we should discard harmful attitudes which can be replaced with positive ones, *i.e.* patience, coolness, firmness and so on. They should be attitudes that reflect confidence and give you the control needed to enjoy the car salesman. Be as economical in your speech as you'd like to be with your money. Refuse to be ruffled or upset by the salesman. Be cool, but don't freeze, of course. Be firm—it's your money. And if you think it's time to walk out, then thank the salesman and walk out. What's there to be afraid of? Put the burden on the salesman! Let him think. Let him earn his money. Let him do the re-considering. Always keep your goal in mind, to buy the car you want at minimum cost and effort.

TONY: You make negotiating sound so easy. Will you try to explain it to us and be specific?

DARRELL:    Tony, I will try. In basic negotiating, there is more to the pattern than just concession-making. In fact, each turn has its own pattern. For the prepared buyer, this pattern has several major steps to be played out. The buyer must PREPARE the seller for the OFFER, then REQUEST the seller to respond. During the response, the buyer must LISTEN then REPLY so the seller knows he has been HEARD before repeating the cycle over again. Each time this verbal contest is played, the buyer and the seller should be closer together in the dealing process. Usually it will take four or five turns to complete the negotiating process. The buyer must remain systematic and remain steadfast with his plan, even if the seller sways (cheats) during the negotiating process.

Here is a possible strategy to take in capturing a used car. First, avoid making any specific offers for the car. Next, tell him that you are a little surprised that he is asking so much for the vehicle. Let the salesman defend his asking price to consume time. Then select another car to test drive in. After returning to the dealership, switch back to the earlier choice, and repeat your statement about the car being over priced. Let the salesman again defend his car. After a short period of time, interrupt the salesman's pitch, with specific information about the car's Blue Book value, and ask the salesman to explain the difference in the two figures. The salesman will discover you are an "in-the-know" buyer, and wait your reply of the car's "true" worth. You need not tell him. Instead, ask for a demo ride. After returning to the dealership, head for your car, thanking the salesman for his time. Of course the salesman will say anything and everything to get you inside his selling room. Act hesitant to this request, but go with him.

Once inside the selling room, you must repeat the same pattern, you must PREPARE the seller for the OFFER, then REQUEST the seller to RESPOND! And this time, during the response, the buyer must LISTEN then REPLY so the seller knows he has been HEARD. After each of these selling plays (where the seller may make demands or request additional cash in the deal), the BUYER must make his own demands to counter the seller. With a little practice this game playing becomes easy to do. That's why I suggest you practice on several dealerships before the real purchase is to take place. "Practice makes perfect" is the motto car salesmen use. That's why they win most of the time!

TONY:        It sounds too complex. What do you mean concessions, offers, etc?

DARRELL:     Tony, each time you negotiate with the salesman (one cycled turn) your offer should benefit your side. To balance you demands, on the salesman, you should include giving in a little (concession). So, to PREPARE the seller for your second offer (and your first concession), you should repeat your earlier offer and let the salesman know you understand how to negotiate with him. After the salesman has HEARD your first offer, then declare your concession (usually some minor option already on the car of choice). Then present your second OFFER, then REQUEST the seller to respond. During the response, the buyer must LISTEN and then REPLY so the seller knows he has been HEARD before trying to repeat the negotiation cycle into the third offer and second concession. Always, acknowledge your second concession before starting your third offer. It sounds difficult but it really can be fun to play this out against any seller of product. Make the seller verbally announce them (your offers and concessions) inside the selling room. The reason is to get the SELLER used to speaking out your offers and concessions in an orderly way. Again, after practicing this form of give and take (you give up little but take much), you'll realize the power you have. After all, you're the carrier of money. Doesn't everyone answer to the dollar!

TONY:          You make it sound too good to be true! Surely the seller will protest?

DARRELL:     Yes, the seller will protest throughout the selling process. He will be quite verbal at times; you need only to be patient and hold your ground. If you did your homework, these sellers will, after playing several of their selling games, get down to verifying their profit (a small one) and sell you the car. The seller's arguments must be dealt with reasonably. If the seller protests and refuses to play the "game" then simply act unpredictable, maybe even head for your car! Any action that seems to end the dealing process will do. After shocking the seller into possibly losing the sale, they will quickly fall into place and continue the selling process. The last OFFER should be the original selling price you believe the car to be worth. Be sure to ask for a full tank of gas and some floor mats.

TONY:          Well, it's that time again. It always seems that we just start having a good time and we have to leave you.

I'd like to thank our guest, Mr. Darrell Parrish, and to remind all of you out there that you can get Mr. Parrish's book, *THE CAR BUYERS ART*—How to Beat the Salesman at His Own Game, at your favorite bookstore.

DARRELL: Thank you, Tony, it's been a pleasure.

TONY: Thanks to all of you out there. And we'll see you again tomorrow at this same time on *Consumer Corner*, station K.A.R.S., now stay tuned for the world news and then Charlie Stone and all your favorite tunes. So long, see ya tomorrow...

*Off the air.*

Say Darrell, now that we're off the air, I'd like to ask you a few other questions if you don't mind, that is...

DARRELL: Of course not, you know we just barely scratched the surface, today. You'll probably be getting questions for the next few days.

TONY: Well, not only from the listeners. I'm thinking of buying something for myself and I'd like to make sure that I'm not going to be paying too much. When I knew you were going to be on the show, I made up a list of questions.

DARRELL: OK, lets hear them.


(CHAPTER 13—questions)

# CHAPTER THIRTEEN

# 13
# THE 36 MOST ASKED QUESTIONS

**Q. WHERE SHOULD I BUY**

**A.** Where you buy a car is important. Because of the amount of money involved, you can justify traveling some to get the best deal, and you shouldn't restrict yourself to local dealers. New car warranty work can be handled by any authorized dealership regardless of where the car was purchased. If you feel that your dealer has given you extra service and consideration in the past, by all means repay the dealer with your loyalty.

But, before you sit down with him to buy a car, have all your *ammunition* with you. Know what your old car is worth and know what your new car has cost the dealer. Most dealers will match any reasonable deal if they know they can make a quick and immediate sale. Using the tactic of shopping elsewhere first and then seeing your favorite dealer last will allow you to do business with people you like, while at the same time keep you from paying more than the lowest possible price.

**Q. Should I know exactly what car I want before I go to the dealer?**

**A.** If you use sources such as *Motor Trend, Changing Times* or *Consumer Reports,* you should be able to make a good choice of cars based on your individual likes, wants and needs. And you'll be able to make that decision in the comfort of your own living room, leisurely and logically instead of the impassioned battlefield of the dealership's showroom, guided by a salesman who might have placed his priority of selling any car above yours. Also, by knowing exactly what car you're going to buy, you'll be able to better control the dealing process by knowing what the dealer paid for the car and what money you'll really *need* to capture that car.

**Q. Can a shy person deal with car salesmen?**

**A.** Shyness is a major problem for some of us. I suggest reading "Shyness," by Mr. Phillip G. Zimbardo, a paperback published in 1954 by Jove Books. This book should assist you in alleviating shyness. It's also suggested a more "dominant" friend go with you to help in your encounter with the salesman.

**Q. Is taking a friend really necessary?**

**A.** Taking a friend along can backfire. Remember your friend's task is specific and to the point: have them ask lots of questions to wear down the salesman's strategies, and to be a "witness." In case you encounter the "unethical" salesman, he/she will play less sales games during the sale. And finally, if the buyer becomes entranced with that car at any price, the friend must physically "kidnap" the buyer and go to the nearest coffee shop for R.R.—*rest and recuperation!* The worst thing that can happen is to buy the wrong car at any price. Cars are too expensive to let this happen to you.

**Q. How can I get a big discount on most cars including those high demand cars?**

**A.** A simple way to capture these cars is to negotiate on a similar car on the lot (a stripped model). Then after spending some time with the salesman and the sales team, adding options to be installed by the dealer, decide to switch to the desired model on the lot that has the options already installed by the factory. Even if you are forced to "order" the car, continue to demand your fair price! The man-hours invested by the sales team will cause the sale to happen. To sweeten the deal let the sales team take small amounts of $50 to $100 back from you (but no more than twice) to allow them a small *victory* for their efforts. But you should close the deal within your "fair" deal figures!

**Q. Why are first time car buyers so vulnerable?**

**A.** First the young car buyer will do almost anything to get into a car. Secondly, he/she is very inexperienced at negotiating. And these people usually have no credit record.

**Q. What mood should the car buyer display with car salesmen and their sales teams?**

**A.** I suggest your mood be continually changing. Start out with an easy going manner until you are face-to-face with the salesman inside his office. As the deal begins to take shape, on paper, your mood should take a more stern position. Continue to follow the salesman's selling routine, allowing only small dollar concessions to cross over the negotiating table. Be patient and the power of your American dollars will play its decisive role and give you a great victory— *the right car at the right price!*

**Q. Do I have to do all the talking to get my deal?**

**A.** Don't haggle needlessly! Often silence works best! Or answer a question with a question to keep the salesman talking. Your best discounts can be captured with silence. If you are silent, the salesman can't tell if he has control of the deal or of you. Keeping the sales team off balance can only be beneficial to you and your pocketbook!

**Q. My last car salesman told me he was a new car salesman. He looked sixty years old! Was he telling the truth?**

**A.** It's very possible. New selling schemes are being tested everyday. Car dealers are hiring retired people to "greet" car buyers on the car lot. Their only goal is to get the buyer inside the salesman's office where others will continue to sale. Win or lose, they are paid a token fee for their efforts. They are not salesmen, they only lead you into a "holding" area for a final close by the *real* sales team inside the dealership.

**Q. Should I outtalk the salesman to get my deal?**

A. Let the salesman do most of the talking. Save your negotiating energies for when the *real* dealing process takes place inside the salesman's office. The salesman listens to all buyer comments for "vital information" that may weaken the buying *position* later on in the deal. Therefore keep your information private! To outtalk a car salesmen, would require you to be one. Car salesmen may train themselves by going to other dealerships, acting like car buyers, to seek out "trade secrets" other salesmen use to take their maximum profits. Role-playing skills require practice. Only the "better" player wins!

**Q. How can I follow the salesman? They talk so fast?**

A. Learn to distinguish small talk from sales talk. The sales team will only use certain language during the sale; all other conversation may be designed to distract you from the facts. The salesman must ask you questions that will qualify you as a real buyer but will also use other topics to gain your trust in him as a "regular" guy. If you stick to a game plan, you'll be able to *sift* through the salesman's attempt to sidetrack you.

**Q. What should I look for in a salesman?**

A. I strongly recommend that you look for the youngest, most inexperienced salesman on the lot. Cling to him. Don't let him go. Chances are that he's not quite the seasoned professional as many of the other salesmen on the lot and at least you'll have an even chance while dealing with this young salesman. However, once inside the salesman's office, you'll be facing the "sales team" members and you'll have to deal with them and their games—so be prepared!

**Q. Why are salesmen nice one moment and rude the next?**

**A.** Often car salesmen work under great stress. If they don't sell X number of cars each month, they may be replaced by a more aggressive salesman. I call this phenomenon Dr. Jekyll/Mr. Hyde! Dr. Jekyll was a good community man who supported community affairs and was concerned for his fellow man. But Mr. Hyde was of another character. Totally selfish, he is capable of almost anything to get what he wants, even at the expense of his fellow man. Mr. Hyde can appear in any salesman's office and one should be prepared to encounter this personality. The best protection will be time. Consume time and appease Mr. Hyde. When the sales team takes control, the dealing process will generally come back to a more businesslike environment. After time has been invested, the buyer should begin to make his demands. The result is that Mr. Hyde will turn back into Dr. Jekyll as the dealing process comes to an end. If this transformation doesn't happen, then I recommend that you leave the premises as fast as you can.

**Q. Why is negotiating a car deal such a pain?**

**A.** Negotiating isn't always easy and nice. The sales team's goal is to make a relatively simple task of buying a car into a complex game to assure the taking of maximum profit. Their (the dealers) complaint is that the consumer is often deceitful—either about their financial position or their trade-in. I challenge this by saying that the seller practices similar skills every day. In this respect, the seller is a professional and as such, really has no competition from these amateur car buyers. Aggressive sellers are very "creative" in their skills. How can the amateur car buyer compete in "story telling"? The buyer should not resort to telling untrue stories, simply follow the sales team's efforts as he would in a game of cards! If things get too painful, by all means "fold your cards" and leave!

**Q. Why must I avoid weekend car buying?**

**A.** The sales team is too busy selling cars to the impulse buyer and shoppers to invest any length of time with you. Impulse buying is the number one downfall for most consumers.

Shopping and buying on separate days is the cure for this ailment. Locating the "right" car and then returning to negotiate the right price seem to reduce impulse buying. If you must buy your car on the weekend, become well versed in this book's concepts and practice them several times. And be prepared to do battle with the "greatest" sellers of all—the car salesman and the sales team.

**Q. How can I check out a service department?**

**A.** Go to the service area where customers are waiting. If there are any complaints to be voiced, these customers will "bend" your ear!

**Q. Why is the end of the month the best time to buy?**

**A.** Every dealership sets goals for each month—an amount of cars to be sold or the amount of profit to be taken. If they haven't yet reached those goals toward the end of the month, they're going to be more willing to bargain with you. A salesman who hasn't met his quota is probably going to hand you your best discounts just to close the deal. Be firm, though, you'll still have to practice *The Car Buyer's Art* techniques, but your rewards (savings) will generally be greater.

**Q. Why do you use "buyer commandments"?**

**A.** To stress a point: Car salesmen are professional sellers and car buyers are amateurs at negotiating their deals. When the buyer learns the game plan and rules salesmen live by, and combines some "buyer" rules of his own, he will have no problem with the sellers on the lot.

**Q. How is car buying a game?**

**A.** A game has a definite set of rules and possible strategies to provide competition and a winner! The players are limited only as to the knowledge of the game's rules and strategies to win against an opponent. In car buying the buyer barely understands the game plan or rules and depends on the salesman to assist in the purchase. There is a sequence of events that car buyers must complete before the sale is made. There are buyer and seller strategies available to compete at the negotiating table in a salesman's office. If you take the time to learn these rules you will enjoy a great victory.

**Q. How do car salesmen learn their trade?**

**A.** By on-the-job experimentation. Say anything and everything to get buyers inside the salesman's office, where the salesman can take over control to complete the sale. Often I acted as though I lost control of the prospective buyer to elicit the skills of sellers higher up on the pecking order. Thus after witnessing this "great" seller's skills—I would adopt them as my own.

**Q. What happens to all those fired or laid-off car salesmen?**

**A.** I have never been asked this question before. I believe the auto industry does a great service to these "fired" salesmen. These sellers usually have less than one year with the dealership's sales team. This experience is valuable to these salesmen's careers for they have learned the difficult selling skills needed to excite and sell. A *prized skill* in any sales job! All these "short-timers" need to do, to continue their sales careers, is to indicate they had worked for a car dealership. I believe these job hunters will be instantly hired in the sales occupation of their choice. A word of warning for veteran car salesmen. You may get an opposite reaction from employers of other sales occupations, for people believe car salesmen are crooks.

**Q. Once a salesman approaches a car of interest, should I make an offer?**

**A.** Please avoid this practice. The real negotiating doesn't start until you are inside the salesman's office. It is better to enter into a negotiating effort without self-imposed limitation, ready to seize any advantage that takes shape during the dealing process. Remember the salesman believes in give-and-take rules: you give and he will take even more cash as the deal comes to a close. "Be patient" should be a car buyer's rule.

**Q. How can I avoid buying a car that has been in a major accident?**

**A.** Obviously, you should have a mechanic friend with you to assist you in evaluating the car's real worth! Also, this friend should drive behind you in another car as you test drive the used car. From this vantage point he can make sure the car drives true to the road, that the frame is straight and the wheels are tracking true to the road.

**Q. Can we spot the unethical salesman?**

**A.** Probably not! You're an amateur car buyer at best. Probably only another car salesman could spot them! And they don't practicularly care to tell anyone!

**Q. Why is time so important?**

**A.** Time usually works in the dealership's favor with the *unprepared* car buyers! With a prepared car buyer, this time becomes worth thousands of discounted dollars. For every man-hour you consume with a dealership—three man-hours are tallied against the sales team. If you spend three hours with the car salesman, the sales team consumes 8-9 hours of trying to close the sale! With this much time used up, the sales team gets a bit nervous about completing the sale. To let the sales team know that a sale can be made only under your conditions can be very unsettling for them. But, with this much time invested, they tend to listen to your demands.

**Q. What's the "real" deal?**

**A.** The *real deal* is the contract ready to be *signed* by the seller and buyer. Anything and everything is negotiable until signing the contract. After signing, though, the sales team will defend its position as final. Not so, in many states, there is a 72-hour cooling off period where both parties can stop the contract. The artistic car buyer will make all his/her demands verbal before the contract is typed up for signature. If you sense you didn't do well—you should leave the dealership prior to signing the contract. Don't feel obligated or sorry—just get out of there! And start over another day, perhaps at another dealership. Sometimes the sales team can take too much (profit) as the deal comes to a close. If this happens to you, you may try to save

the deal and demand these extras removed or simply leave
and do business elsewhere!

**Q. What about the dealers who advertise "low interest"
financing?**

**A.** In using the dealership's financing, one usually is considering
the convenience factor—how easy it is to deal with just
one group of people. Sort of one-stop shopping. And if
the dealer offers a low interest loan—so much the better.
But first consider that in many cases "low interest loan"
usually applies to only specific cars ON the lot or cars that
are sold at "sticker price." I recommend concentrating on
getting the best possible price first, then even with a slightly
higher rate of interest, you may end up with the better deal.
However, if you've secured a loan on your own at the same
rates as the dealer offered, you come out a double winner!
Going for the "right" price becomes easier.

**Q. How can I reduce the "games" salesmen play?**

**A.** Take a friend with you to assist! His/her presence as a
witness, makes even an unethical salesman nervous. The
problem here is that the "friend" could be turned against
the buyer and actually assist the salesman in the deal. So
make sure your friend is well aware of the task of keeping
the salesman off balance during the dealing process, and
they will become worth their weight in "Gold" if the deal
goes sour and you need "pulling" out of the deal. Yes, they
should actually "kidnap" you from the sales office and take
you to the nearest coffee shop for a little R&R—rest and
recouperation. Please note: In most cases, you can not
eliminate the sales games. You should simply flow with them,
keeping in mind your goal of getting the right car at the
right price!

**Q. Are used cars really safety checked?**

**A.** In most cases a brief survey of the condition of the car
is made. If a faulty transmission is discovered, the dealer
may choose to defer repairs until the car is sold. Then under
a limited warranty the repair bill will be split with the buyer.
If the repair falls past the warranty time limit, the dealer

has successfully transferred the problem to the buyer at no cost to them (the dealership).

**Q. Is confusing the salesman ethical and fair?**

**A.** What's ethical and fair? Have you ever played cards with someone or a group and flashed your hand to them prior to competing? Isn't the game over for you? The person who studies his opponent or adversary for clues to their strategies surely has the advantage over one who deals in pure chance. To be an equal to the car salesman—you must know the game plan and rules they live by. Then and only then can you expect to compete as a *true* adversary.

**Q. Why do salesman continually ask for more money during the selling process?**

**A.** You must realize that the main job of the sales team is to take any and all additional profits that are available beyond the selling price of the car. They do this to the buyer first by "shocking" them in a lock-up fashion. Then by pressuring the buyer several times during the deal for additional cash. By using different salesmen, the sales team can take more profits over a period of time. Individual sellers are not as efficient as the team in total. Be aware of this practice of "bumping." But let them try anyway, give them the false sense of being in control. Then, you close the deal when you want to, on your terms!

**Q. Why are so many women selling cars today?**

**A.** Women are expanding their skills in the traditionally man's world. Unfortunately for the consumer, these women sellers are taking even more profits for the dealership. Women as the front-line troopers often "steer" the male buyer— by keeping him off balance or at the very least by keeping him *timid* and *shy* in demanding his points. I ask the male consumer to share the negotiating duties (especially near the end of the negotiating process) with his wife or a female friend. She becomes a *natural* adversary to the woman seller. When she discovers the money at risk.

**Q. What is the purpose of the papermill inside the salesman's office? What is the papermill?**

**A.** The papermill is the use of paperwork to control the buyer and the salesman through a sequence of events so the sales team is assured maximum profit as the deal comes to a close. Buyers are "walked" through the trade-in worth, price of the new car, down payment required, and monthly payments—if financing is to be arranged. The sales team can repeatedly go through these segments to capture maximum profit prior to the manager's decision to close the deal. The papermill is a complex, but orderly, way of placing on paper the "real deal" between the seller and buyer.

**Q.** **Will the salesman "hold" my check for a couple of weeks so I have time to decide if that's the car I really want?**

**A.** If you write a check on the weekend to hold a car, chances are that check was cashed on the following Monday. This way the dealership has a way to *hold* you to your end of the deal! Make sure you get a receipt and that it is refundable if you purchase elsewhere. Also, try to post date the check. This may give you time to stop the check before this situation could turn for the worst.

**Q.** **As the dealing process comes to a close, must I commit to that deal? Is it final?**

**A.** No for both questions. If the dealer has taken too much profit during the dealing process, you can walk out of the deal. Dealing with these sellers is complex; they prefer it that way! If you are not competing well with them, consider the experience as "practice" and go. Do not get emotional with these sellers', just take your money and do your business elsewhere!!

**Q.** **These car salesmen gave me a discount, they must be on my side!**

**A.** It could be a fictitious discount! That is, the salesman may have just increased the asking price and then discounted it back down to its *original* asking price to make you feel you're getting a *discount* and will not ask for more *money* off. This is popular in used cars, but can be seen on the new cars in the form of Additional Dealer Markup Stickers. Please note: Car salesmen must talk to a lot of prospective buyers before closing a sale. A common ratio is two sales

217

for every 15-20 contacts. The salesman must take maximum profit from these "now" buyers just to make a living. The salesman can appear to be the friendliest person you've encountered, but takes excessive profits from the buyers in the meantime. Discounting is common in the auto industry, but is it a real discount? Only the prepared buyer can tell.

**Q. Should I bid for a car that has already been sold?**

A. I suggest you stay away from bidding for cars that have already been sold. Dealerships can place "sold" signs on several of their "high" demand cars to get even more money from the consumer anxious to take immediate delivery. In reality they are not sold, but may be on "hold"; the dealer is holding them for the highest "bidder." Go elsewhere where they play less "games" with the consumer.

# DO YOUR FRIENDS AND RELATIVES A FAVOR!

Now that you are an EXPERT CAR BUYER, why not spread the word! Your friends will continue to ask your advice on car buying. They will listen to every word you say. Save your friends a ton-of-money by giving them a copy of THE CAR BUYER'S ART. It is a gift that cannot be equalled, for the buying strategies *revealed in this book cannot be learned or found anywhere else!*

Introducing a newly released video tape with party appeal (see reverse page). A video tape that prepares a buyer with "consumer punch!" Invite your friends and relatives over for a VCR PARTY! Everyone has a "story" on how they buy their cars. You'll be amazed how receptive your guests will be to your VCR PARTY IDEA!

Order *extra copies* of THE CAR BUYER'S ART for only $4.95 plus $1.00 shipping & handling. Just fill out the below coupon, mail it, and Book Express will send you, along with your book order, a free *audio cassette* of the author, Mr. Parrish, chatting on a local radio station.

If the VCR PARTY sounds like an excellent idea, send $25.00, check or money order, and you will get four (4) copies of THE CAR BUYER'S ART to present to your party guests free from BOOK EXPRESS. It's like getting a video tape free, when you consider the four book offer is valued at $24.00. Just fill out the below coupon, mail it, with your check or money order to:

Yes, rush me _____ copies of your book, THE CAR BUYER'S ART and its companion audio cassette. Yes, I like the VCR PARTY IDEA! Send me _____ copies of your video tape, THE CAR BUYER'S GUIDE, including the four (4) free book offer with purchase. I have enclosed the correct amount in check or money order to fulfill my order with Book Express.

Number of books at $5.95 postage paid is    _____.
Number of video tapes at $24.00 ppd is    _____.
Total due by check or money order is    _____.

Name_____

Address_____

City_____ State_____ Zip_____

# THE CAR BUYER'S GUIDE

## HOW TO
## BEAT THE SALESMAN
## AT HIS OWN GAME!

. . . The Prepared

## WIN!

BASED ON THE BOOK
"THE CAR BUYER'S ART"
by Darrell Parrish

For decades, car salesmen have been free to practice their craft on the American Public. Today, consumers complain about becoming victims of these infamous sellers. Car dealers continue their profit taking by pressuring the salesmen via complicated courses. These sellers have become so professional, so proficient, at parting you from your money that few car buyers survive the encounter.

THE CAR BUYER'S GUIDE . . . HOW TO BEAT THE SALESMAN AT HIS OWN GAME will change all this. It's as easy as popping this tape into your VCR player, sitting back and watching the actors play out the scenario for you. The sellers can use every trick in the book, but to no avail. The video tape will show you how to outmaneuver these sellers at every corner for an easy victory and big savings!

THE CAR BUYER'S GUIDE . . . will safeguard millions of consumer dollars from the "greedy" hands of car salesmen. This video has party appeal, entertainment, and valuable information if you are in the market for a car. This video is a must. For the first time, you will "leap" for the chance to encounter a car salesman. You'll have fun practicing on a few local dealerships to measure your new-found negotiating power prior to the actual purchase. You'll quickly discover the big dollar savings is yours for the taking! And most important of all, you'll get to WIN — a thrilling achievement to savor for years to come!

1988/ Color/ Approx 58 minutes running time.

## ISBN 0-929406-00-1

# DO YOUR FRIENDS AND RELATIVES A FAVOR!

Now that you are an EXPERT CAR BUYER, why not spread the word! Your friends will continue to ask your advice on car buying. They will listen to every word you say. Save your friends a ton-of-money by giving them a copy of THE CAR BUYER'S ART. It is a gift that cannot be equalled, for the buying strategies *revealed in this book cannot be learned or found anywhere else!*

Introducing a newly released video tape with party appeal (see reverse page). A video tape that prepares a buyer with "consumer punch!" Invite your friends and relatives over for a VCR PARTY! Everyone has a "story" on how they buy their cars. You'll be amazed how receptive your guests will be to your VCR PARTY IDEA!

Order *extra copies* of THE CAR BUYER'S ART for only $4.95 plus $1.00 shipping & handling. Just fill out the below coupon, mail it, and Book Express will send you, along with your book order, a free *audio cassette* of the author, Mr. Parrish, chatting on a local radio station.

If the VCR PARTY sounds like an excellent idea, send $25.00, check or money order, and you will get four (4) copies of THE CAR BUYER'S ART to present to your party guests free from BOOK EXPRESS. It's like getting a video tape free, when you consider the four book offer is valued at $24.00. Just fill out the below coupon, mail it, with your check or money order to:

---

Yes, rush me _____ copies of your book, THE CAR BUYER'S ART and its companion audio cassette. Yes, I like the VCR PARTY IDEA! Send me _____ copies of your video tape, THE CAR BUYER'S GUIDE, including the four (4) free book offer with purchase. I have enclosed the correct amount in check or money order to fulfill my order with Book Express.

Number of books at $5.95 postage paid is _____.
Number of video tapes at $24.00 ppd is _____.
Total due by check or money order is _____.

Name_____

Address_____

City_____ State_____ Zip_____

# THE CAR BUYER'S GUIDE

### HOW TO BEAT THE SALESMAN AT HIS OWN GAME!

. . . The Prepared

**WIN!**

BASED ON THE BOOK
"THE CAR BUYER'S ART"
by Darrell Parrish

For decades, car salesmen have been free to practice their craft on the American Public. Today, consumers complain about becoming victims of these infamous sellers! Car dealers continue their profit-taking by training their sales teams via "special" satellite courses. These sellers have become so proficient, so professional, at parting you from your money that few car buyers survive the encounter.

THE CAR BUYER'S GUIDE . . . HOW TO BEAT THE SALESMAN AT HIS OWN GAME will change all this. It's as easy as popping this tape into your VCR player, sitting back and watching the actions play out the scenario for you. The sellers can use every trick in the book, but to no avail, the video tape will show you how to outmaneuver these sellers at every corner for an easy victory and big savings!

THE CAR BUYER'S GUIDE . . . will safeguard millions of consumer dollars from the "greedy" hands of car salesmen. This video has party appeal, entertainment, and valuable information. If you are in the market for a car. This video is a must. For the first time, you will "leap" for the chance to encounter a car salesman. You'll have fun practicing on a few local dealerships to measure your new-found negotiating power prior to the actual purchase. You'll quickly discover the big dollar savings is yours for the taking! And most important of all, you'll get to WIN — a thrilling achievement to savor for years to come!

1988/Color/Approx 58 minutes running time.

**ISBN 0-929406-00-1**

Distributed by Rodgers Productions, N. Hollywood, CA. Copyright Darrell Parrish and Herb Rodgers. All rights reserved. Printed in U.S.A. Warning: Licensed for non-commercial private exhibition. Any form of public performance, other use, copying, reproduction, or broadcast of this video in whole or in part, in any manner is prohibited and violates applicable copyright laws. The offender will be subject to severe criminal penalties (Title 17, United States Code, Section 501 & 506).

# DO YOUR FRIENDS AND RELATIVES A FAVOR!

Now that you are an EXPERT CAR BUYER, why not spread the word! Your friends will continue to ask your advice on car buying. They will listen to every word you say. Save your friends a ton-of-money by giving them a copy of THE CAR BUYER'S ART. It is a gift that cannot be equalled, for the buying strategies *revealed in this book cannot be learned or found anywhere else!*

Introducing a newly released video tape with party appeal (see reverse page). A video tape that prepares a buyer with "consumer punch!" Invite your friends and relatives over for a VCR PARTY! Everyone has a "story" on how they buy their cars. You'll be amazed how receptive your guests will be to your VCR PARTY IDEA!

Order *extra copies* of THE CAR BUYER'S ART for only $4.95 plus $1.00 shipping & handling. Just fill out the below coupon, mail it, and Book Express will send you, along with your book order, a free *audio cassette* of the author, Mr. Parrish, chatting on a local radio station.

If the VCR PARTY sounds like an excellent idea, send $25.00, check or money order, and you will get four (4) copies of THE CAR BUYER'S ART to present to your party guests free from BOOK EXPRESS. It's like getting a video tape free, when you consider the four book offer is valued at $24.00. Just fill out the below coupon, mail it, with your check or money order to:

---

Yes, rush me _____ copies of your book, THE CAR BUYER'S ART and its companion audio cassette. Yes, I like the VCR PARTY IDEA! Send me _____ copies of your video tape, THE CAR BUYER'S GUIDE, including the four (4) free book offer with purchase. I have enclosed the correct amount in check or money order to fulfill my order with Book Express.

Number of books at $5.95 postage paid is _____.
Number of video tapes at $24.00 ppd is _____.
Total due by check or money order is _____.
Name_____
Address_____
City_____ State_____ Zip_____

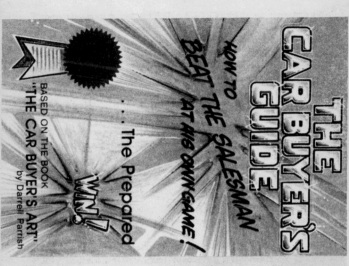

# THE CAR BUYER'S GUIDE

## HOW TO BEAT THE SALESMAN AT HIS OWN GAME!

... The Prepared WIN!

BASED ON THE BOOK
"THE CAR BUYER'S ART"
by Darrell Parrish

For decades, car salesmen have been free to practice their craft on the American Public. Today, consumers complain about becoming victims of these infamous sellers! Car dealers continue their profit-taking by turning their sales teams via "special" satellite courses, these sellers have become so professional, so proficient, at parting you from your money that few car buyers survive the encounter.

THE CAR BUYER'S GUIDE . . . HOW TO BEAT THE SALESMAN AT HIS OWN GAME, will change all this. It's as easy as popping this tape into your VCR player, sitting back, and watching the actors play out the scenario for you. The seller can, and every trick in the book, but no one deal, the video tape will show you how to outmaneuver these sellers at every corner for an easy victory and big savings.

THE CAR BUYER'S GUIDE . . . will safeguard millions of consumer dollars from the "greedy" hands of car salesmen. This video has party appeal, entertainment, and valuable information. If you are in the market for a car, this video is a must. For the first time, you will "leap" for the chance to encounter a car salesman. You'll have fun practicing on a few local dealerships to measure your new-found negotiating power prior to the actual purchase. You'll quickly discover the big dollar savings is yours for the taking. And most important of all, you'll get to WIN --- a thrilling achievement to savor for years to come!

1988/Color/Approx. 58 minutes running time.

ISBN 0-929406-00-1

# DO YOUR FRIENDS AND RELATIVES A FAVOR!

Now that you are an EXPERT CAR BUYER, why not spread the word! Your friends will continue to ask your advice on car buying. They will listen to every word you say. Save your friends a ton-of-money by giving them a copy of THE CAR BUYER'S ART. It is a gift that cannot be equalled, for the buying strategies *revealed in this book cannot be learned or found anywhere else!*

Introducing a newly released video tape with party appeal (see reverse page). A video tape that prepares a buyer with "consumer punch!" Invite your friends and relatives over for a VCR PARTY! Everyone has a "story" on how they buy their cars. You'll be amazed how receptive your guests will be to your VCR PARTY IDEA!

Order *extra copies* of THE CAR BUYER'S ART for only $4.95 plus $1.00 shipping & handling. Just fill out the below coupon, mail it, and Book Express will send you, along with your book order, a free *audio cassette* of the author, Mr. Parrish, chatting on a local radio station.

If the VCR PARTY sounds like an excellent idea, send $25.00, check or money order, and you will get four (4) copies of THE CAR BUYER'S ART to present to your party guests free from BOOK EXPRESS. It's like getting a video tape free, when you consider the four book offer is valued at $24.00. Just fill out the below coupon, mail it, with your check or money order to:

---

Yes, rush me _____ copies of your book, THE CAR BUYER'S ART and its companion audio cassette. Yes, I like the VCR PARTY IDEA! Send me _____ copies of your video tape, THE CAR BUYER'S GUIDE, including the four (4) free book offer with purchase. I have enclosed the correct amount in check or money order to fulfill my order with Book Express.

Number of books at $5.95 postage paid is _____.
Number of video tapes at $24.00 ppd is _____.
Total due by check or money order is _____.

Name_____

Address_____

City_____ State_____ Zip_____

# THE CAR BUYER'S GUIDE

## HOW TO BEAT THE SALESMAN AT HIS OWN GAME!

## . . . The Prepared WIN!

BASED ON THE BOOK "THE CAR BUYER'S ART" by Darrell Parrish

For decades, car salesmen have been free to practice their craft on the American Public. Today, consumers complain about becoming victims of these infamous sellers! Car dealers continue their profit-taking by training their sales teams to "special" satellite courses. These sellers have become so professional, so proficient, at parting you from your money that few car buyers survive the encounter.

THE CAR BUYER'S GUIDE . . . HOW TO BEAT THE SALESMAN AT HIS OWN GAME will change all this. It's as easy as popping this tape into your VCR player, sitting back, and watching the actors play out the scenarios for you. The reality soon, use every trick in the book, but to no avail. This video tape will show you how to outmaneuver these sellers at every corner for an easy victory and big savings!

THE CAR BUYER'S GUIDE . . . will safeguard millions of consumer dollars from the "greedy" hands of car salesmen. This video has party appeal, entertainment, and valuable information if you are in the market for a car. This video is a must. For the first time, you will "leap" for the chance to encounter a car salesman. You'll have fun practicing on a few local dealerships to measure your new-found negotiating power prior to the actual purchase. You'll quickly discover the big dollar savings is yours for the taking! And most important of all, you'll get to WIN — a thrilling achievement to savor for years to come!

1988/Color/Approx. 58 minutes running time.

ISBN 0-929406-00-1

# DO YOUR FRIENDS AND RELATIVES A FAVOR!

Now that you are an EXPERT CAR BUYER, why not spread the word! Your friends will continue to ask your advice on car buying. They will listen to every word you say. Save your friends a ton-of-money by giving them a copy of THE CAR BUYER'S ART. It is a gift that cannot be equalled, for the buying strategies *revealed in this book cannot be learned or found anywhere else!*

Introducing a newly released video tape with party appeal (see reverse page). A video tape that prepares a buyer with "consumer punch!" Invite your friends and relatives over for a VCR PARTY! Everyone has a "story" on how they buy their cars. You'll be amazed how receptive your guests will be to your VCR PARTY IDEA!

Order *extra copies* of THE CAR BUYER'S ART for only $4.95 plus $1.00 shipping & handling. Just fill out the below coupon, mail it, and Book Express will send you, along with your book order, a free *audio cassette* of the author, Mr. Parrish, chatting on a local radio station.

If the VCR PARTY sounds like an excellent idea, send $25.00, check or money order, and you will get four (4) copies of THE CAR BUYER'S ART to present to your party guests free from BOOK EXPRESS. It's like getting a video tape free, when you consider the four book offer is valued at $24.00. Just fill out the below coupon, mail it, with your check or money order to:

Yes, rush me _____ copies of your book, THE CAR BUYER'S ART and its companion audio cassette. Yes, I like the VCR PARTY IDEA! Send me _____ copies of your video tape, THE CAR BUYER'S GUIDE, including the four (4) free book offer with purchase. I have enclosed the correct amount in check or money order to fulfill my order with Book Express.

Number of books at $5.95 postage paid is       _____.
Number of video tapes at $24.00 ppd is       _____.
Total due by check or money order is       _____.

Name_____

Address_____

City_____ State_____ Zip_____

# DO YOUR FRIENDS AND RELATIVES
# A FAVOR!

Now that you are an EXPERT CAR BUYER, why not spread the word! Your friends will continue to ask your advice on car buying. They will listen to every word you say. Save your friends a ton-of-money by giving them a copy of THE CAR BUYER'S ART. It is a gift that cannot be equalled, for the buying strategies *revealed in this book cannot be learned or found anywhere else!*

Introducing a newly released video tape with party appeal (see reverse page). A video tape that prepares a buyer with "consumer punch!" Invite your friends and relatives over for a VCR PARTY! Everyone has a "story" on how they buy their cars. You'll be amazed how receptive your guests will be to your VCR PARTY IDEA!

Order *extra copies* of THE CAR BUYER'S ART for only $4.95 plus $1.00 shipping & handling. Just fill out the below coupon, mail it, and Book Express will send you, along with your book order, a free *audio cassette* of the author, Mr. Parrish, chatting on a local radio station.

If the VCR PARTY sounds like an excellent idea, send $25.00, check or money order, and you will get four (4) copies of THE CAR BUYER'S ART to present to your party guests free from BOOK EXPRESS. It's like getting a video tape free, when you consider the four book offer is valued at $24.00. Just fill out the below coupon, mail it, with your check or money order to:

---

Yes, rush me _____ copies of your book, THE CAR BUYER'S ART and its companion audio cassette. Yes, I like the VCR PARTY IDEA! Send me _____ copies of your video tape, THE CAR BUYER'S GUIDE, including the four (4) free book offer with purchase. I have enclosed the correct amount in check or money order to fulfill my order with Book Express.

    Number of books at $5.95 postage paid is     _____.
    Number of video tapes at $24.00 ppd is     _____.
    Total due by check or money order is     _____.
Name_____
Address_____
City_____ State_____ Zip_____

# THE CAR BUYER'S GUIDE

## HOW TO BEAT THE SALESMAN AT HIS OWN GAME!

. . . . The Prepared WIN !

BASED ON THE BOOK
"THE CAR BUYER'S ART"
by Darrell Parrish

For decades, car salesmen have been free to practice their craft on the American Public. Today, consumers complain about becoming victims of these infamous sellers. Car dealers continue their profit taking by training their sales teams via 'special' satellite courses. These sellers have become so professional, so proficient, at parting you from your money that few car buyers survive the encounter.

THE CAR BUYER'S GUIDE . . . HOW TO BEAT THE SALESMAN AT HIS OWN GAME will change all this. It's as easy as popping this tape into your VCR player, sitting back and watching the actors play out the scenario for you. The sellers can use every trick in the book, but no avail, the video tape will show you how to outmaneuver these sellers at every corner for an easy victory and big savings!

THE CAR BUYER'S GUIDE . . . will safeguard millions of consumer dollars from the 'greedy' hands of car salesmen. This video has party appeal, entertainment, and valuable information if you are in the market for a car. This video is a must. For the first time, you will 'leap' for the chance to encounter a car salesman. You'll have fun practicing on a few local dealerships to measure your new-found negotiating power prior to the actual purchase. You'll quickly discover the big dollar savings is yours for the taking. And most important of all, you'll get to WIN — a thrilling achievement to savor for years to come!

1988/Color/Approx. 58 minutes running time.

## ISBN 0-929406-00-1